Physicians,
Law,
& Ethics

Carleton B. Chapman

Physicians, Law, and Ethics

PHYSICIANS, LAW, AND ETHICS

Carleton B. Chapman

New York University Press
NEW YORK & LONDON
1984

Library of Congress Cataloging in Publication Data

Chapman, Carleton, 1915–
    Physicians, law, and ethics.

    Includes bibliographical references and index.
    1. Medical ethics—History.   2. Medical laws and
legislation—History.   I. Title.   [DNLM: 1. Ethics,
Medical.   2. Legislation, Medical.   W50 C465p]
R724.C45 1984   174'.2   84-2130
ISBN 0-8147-1392-0 (alk. paper)
ISBN 0-8147-1393-9 (pbk.)

Book design by Ken Venezio

To HRH

I know that history at all times draws the strangest consequence from remotest cause.

—T. S. ELIOT, *Murder in the Cathedral*

Contents

Acknowledgments   xi

Introduction   xiii

1 · Before the Greeks and Romans   1

2 · The Greeks: Hippocratic Medicine and Ethics   15

3 · Roman Influence and the Dark Ages   35

4 · The Common Law of Malpractice and London's
Medical Guilds   49

5 · From Thomas Percival to Informed Consent   75

6 · Codes and Principles of Ethics of the American
Medical Association, 1847–1957   103

7 · The Future: Ethical Profession or Politicized Industry?   125

Conclusion   145

Notes   149

Index   183

Acknowledgments

In the effort to understand the medical profession's weaknesses and strengths from its beginning to its present state, I have sought the counsel of many expert and well-qualified individuals. My gratitude for their advice and instruction is immense, and it is a pleasure to acknowledge some of them by name. They include Rabbi Levi Olan of Dallas and the late Rabbi Bernard Bamberger of New York; many colleagues at Albert Einstein College of Medicine; Professor George P. Cuttino, medievalist, of Emory University; and Professor Alan Watson, legal historian and classicist, formerly of Edinburgh and now at the University of Pennsylvania. I am especially grateful to Ruth Anshen for her encouragement, staunch idealism, and suggestions, which were the basis for the final chapter. For translation of Scribonius Largus' introduction I turned to Dr. Jeffrey Hamilton, then of Emory and now at Tufts University. For translation and interpretation of Kosarev's article in Russian I am indebted to Dr. Ilya Kreynin of Brooklyn.

In addition to these authorities and counselors I sought the advice of many others, too numerous to be listed, usually on specific points. They included ancient historians, classicists, archaeologists, and especially qualified members of the medical profession. As for librarians, they also are too numerous to be listed. They were uniformly generous, competent, and good company. Special thanks are owed to three secretaries who, over more than a decade, labored uncomplainingly through innumerable revisions and who managed to keep sources and quantities of reference material in reasonable order. They are Brigitta Payne, Shirley Porter, and Jennie DiLoreto.

I should be very remiss if I failed to mention the interest and encouragement of my colleagues and the Board of Directors at the Commonwealth Fund from 1973 to 1980. The setting they provided was a uniquely congenial one for scholarly effort as well as for the imaginative use of private funds in support of higher education.

For use of materials I had published in *The Pharos* and *Perspectives in Biology and Medicine* I thank the publishers. A quotation from *Murder in the Cathedral*, copyright 1935 by Harcourt Brace Jovanovich, Inc.; renewed 1963 by T. S. Eliot is reprinted by permission of the publisher. Excerpts from a January 31, 1983 review by John Updike in *The New Yorker*, © 1983, by John Updike, are reprinted by permission.

Introduction

The noble profession of medicine, as the second millennium
A.D. nears its conclusion, is in trouble. The reasons are numerous and their relative importance is debatable, but one of
the most important is that the profession, after centuries of
temporizing and rationalizing, now seeks to become ethical in
the fullest sense of the word. Closely related to this is that
medicine must have the courage to define itself in terms of its
very special obligations and intellectual uniqueness. It is not
simply bioscience or a special sort of art, as some would have
us believe.

Organized medicine for generations has seen little reason
to probe its mission, with counsel from appropriate lay groups,
in the humanitarian and genuinely ethical sense, or to review
its long history in relentlessly realistic terms. The problem
has been that "whenever the historically minded viewed . . .
medicine's past . . . they perceived dedication, greatness and
progress."[1] Their perceptions are correct as far as they go,
but there have also been negative aspects, including avarice,
self-deception, pettiness, and implacable opposition to change.

The official assertion in the first half of the twentieth century was that medicine was an ethical profession, one that

policed itself and vigorously punished its own wrongdoers. As for ethics per se, the official Principles of Medical Ethics of the American Medical Association (AMA) was the near-perfect treatment, a thoroughly adequate guide to professional conduct. But in the late nineteen-forties and early fifties the AMA's policies became suspect to many American physicians. In the background were the pitched battles between the AMA and the federal government, mostly concerning proposals to establish federally backed health insurance.[2] The impact of these events on American physicians, especially those just entering the profession, is not easily documented, but it was beyond question very great. Many strongly disapproved of the campaign on behalf of the AMA against what was labelled "socialized medicine" by a public relations firm. But they disapproved mostly in silence. It was, at the time, necessary to be a member in good standing of local, state, and national medical societies and associations in order to be admitted to hospital staffs and to obtain malpractice insurance. Lacking such membership and eligibility for insurance, one became a non-person where the medical profession was concerned.

During this stressful period there were no even-handed and impartial efforts to view the events in any sort of historical context and perspective. There were, however, a fair number of lay critics who held that the medical profession was doomed because, for strictly political reasons, it had abandoned its traditional commitment to the exemplary ethical principles that were allegedly contained in the *Oath* attributed to Hippocrates. It was now conducting itself as a labor union, and a ruthless and unprincipled one at that.

The judgment of such critics was, however, seriously flawed. Had they, in the first place, read with care the *Oath* attributed to Hippocrates, they would have found it virtually incomprehensible as an ethical guide. Had they also delved into the social and political maneuverings and machinations of medical guilds across two millennia they would, reluctantly perhaps, have had to concede that the AMA in the late forties was doing no more than following the profession-oriented traditions that have usually characterized the actions of medicine's spokesman organizations since the Golden Age of Greece. A few short periods of official conduct that were generous and altruistic can be identified: for example, the AMA's position on national health insurance from 1912 to 1919. That remarkable episode was followed by a swing back to the ultraconservatism to which organized medicine has clung until very recently.

It is unfortunate that the behavior of organized medicine is so often criticized out of historical context. It has, at times, been fighting for its very life; this has to be viewed, at the very least, as an extenuating circumstance. The sentimentalization of the remarkable ancient Greek civilization routinely obscures the fact that the notion of consumer's rights, backed by law, would probably have been incomprehensible to Greek authorities and Hippocratic physicians in the fifth or fourth centuries B.C. The tribal past of Greece left its mark on important Greek social and political institutions, including craft clans such as the Asklepiadai (physicians and healers), the Homeridai (singers and minstrels), the Iamidai (prophets), and the Talthybiadai (heralds). The function of such organizations was not only to transmit the secret lore of the past; it was also to protect the craft's monopoly and other prerogatives against interlopers. At their induction, new members swore to protect the honor and dignity of the clan above all else.

The concept of a principle of professional ethics focussing on the patient was not to appear fully formed until near our own time, although it was voiced in principle by the pre-exilic prophet Amos well before the Golden Age of Greece. Something like it appears in Luke 12:48 and in Roman writings of the first century A.D. but only very transiently and in modified form.

There is little evidence of the patient-centered ethic in the codes and pronouncements of medical bodies from the days of imperial Rome to our own, although during the latter part of the period, modest ethical principles occasionally influenced decisions by English and American jurists as the law of malpractice took shape. The legal profession as an organized body has all along functioned as has medicine: its primary concern has been its own political and fiscal welfare. It must, however, be noted that over the last several centuries jurists have been more prolific and creative in their writings about professional ethics than have members of the medical profession.

The battles of the late forties extended into the mid-sixties, when the Medicare and Medicaid amendments became law. The year (1965) seems to have been the signal for a vast upsurge of interest in professional ethics in general. As for the medical profession, the impetus may be said to have been no more than an effort on its part to repair its undeniably damaged public image. This, however, was probably the least of it. Medicine as a profession is today confronted with the urgent necessity to face up to its major dilemmas, instead of tabling them sine die or avoiding them by resort to pious subterfuge.

What has brought about this great change? The easiest answers are the decline since the nineteen-twenties of laissez faire, and the growth of consumerism since World War II. The full explanation, however, is probably much more fundamental, subtle, and complex; it can hardly be described solely in terms of standard sociopolitical tenets. However this may be, the essence of the change is that the medical profession can no longer function primarily for its own benefit: its first obligation is to those who require its services, and it must revise its ethics accordingly. This is one inference to be drawn from an assertion made a quarter of a century ago: "One can never get very far from the fact that medicine is directly concerned with human beings and represents a sort of final common pathway down which some scientific principles must travel in order finally to be applied to man himself."[3] It also leads directly to the second dilemma, which has to do with the grievously difficult business of redefining medicine in terms of its legitimate content and structure: is it hard science, art, soft science, or some sort of amorphous compound? Is it an insensitive conduit between science and patient? Or is it a sensitive screen between them, selecting and transmitting only those items that, for each patient, are reasonably certain to be of benefit and not harmful? This particular dilemma has arisen as a result of the failure of the nineteenth-century expectation that medicine and bioscience are, or must soon become, one and the same.

In a sense, the powerful intermingling of some aspects of science and some aspects of what we loosely call the humanities has produced the crisis of identity. It is not to be laid to rest, moreover, by shallow generalities such as the thoughtless claim that medicine is a mixture of art and science, more the former than the latter. Much more helpful are the dialogues now taking place between members of the medical profession and moral philosophers, precipitated in part by the elaboration of a number of life-supporting techniques that make it possible to keep alive indefinitely patients who would otherwise expire quickly. The meeting of the minds of physicians and philosophers has not been without rancor, impatience, and occasional resort to sophistry. But it may, in the end, result in the development of a forum of a sort that has not previously existed in medical circles.

It is abundantly clear that although the tribal concept of craft and craft-oriented codes has endured over an astonishingly long period, it has now had its day. The concept has consistently had the effect of blocking or retarding efforts to resolve the medical profession's dominant dilemmas, efforts that possess implications for restructuring many aspects of the profession's procedure and outlook, beginning with all levels of the educational process that leads to licensure, but also extending into the system within which patient and doctor relate to each other.

Depending on the outcome is medicine's social status in the future. Will it retain its professional status and special prerogatives? Or will it prove to be unable to adapt to the requirements of the late second, and the third, millenniums A.D., and be forced, as a consequence, to revert to the status of a trade or craft?

Physicians, Law, and Ethics

1 · Before the Greeks
and Romans

The record of human activity, including the archaeologic, shows beyond much doubt that the role of the healer of disease and injury is a necessary one even in the most primitive societies. It is a role that must be played; the player is usually an individual who possesses, or is thought to possess, appropriate talents and qualifications. The analogue of the physician and surgeon in modern Western society is to be found, in other forms and with various titles, in most other societies, from the most primitive to the most complex.[1]

Because of its abstract nature, regulation of the healing calling by means of law and ethical admonition is not discernible until after the development of writing in Mesopotamia, about 3000 B.C.[2] Legal regulation apparently came first and followed patterns of customary law that were designed to settle many kinds of disputes between individuals. One such pattern was that which provided compensation for personal injury resulting from the action (or, later, the inaction) of another person or persons. This, the analogue of modern tort law, is a central focus of all ancient law,[3] and under it the healer came to be held to account, under some circumstances, for injury resulting from his management of patients.

But what of the beginnings of ethical thought? It is convenient, as a first approach to this difficult topic, to note that many ancient philosophers made little distinction between legal obligation and moral, or ethical, duty. It would, however, be very misleading to assume that in our own time law and ethics are one and the same thing. For present purposes we may view ethics, in a free society at least, as concerned with rules that are beyond the province of law, in that they summon the individual to actions that are nobler, and usually more altruistic, than those required by law. Legal requirements, in contrast, are in a sense minimal; in some instances (for example, the common law of negligence), the standard of performance required by law is by design mediocre. Ethical standards, to the contrary, require the best performance the individual can, by virtue of training and natural endowment, deliver.

Sumer and Babylon. The Sumerians of Mesopotamia wrote no history as such, but they left behind a vast legacy of "firsts" inscribed on clay tablets in cuneiform script. Theirs was the first urban society, the first palace economy, and the first recorded example of what Walter Ullmann calls the descending thesis of government.[4] And it was a Sumerian scribe who made the first record of ethical thought, attributed to Urukagina, ruler of Lagash, a Sumerian city-state. The date was approximately 2350 B.C., and the ethical concepts had to do not with healing but with restoration of justice and freedom to the citizens of Lagash. The king also showed great concern for the plight of widows, orphans, and the poor generally; concerns that by their nature belong in the ethical category. No law bound the king to show such concerns; he could, under the prevailing system, have exploited the people, both rich and poor, quite legally, as many ancient rulers were wont to do. But Urakagina, acting under unknown influences, reached beyond the law for excellence in a moral and ethical sense.[5] Ironically, his good intent did not prevent him from going down to utter defeat ten years after he became king.

In succeeding centuries other Sumerian rulers routinely claimed in prologues to law codes to have been on the side of truth, law and order, justice and freedom, and mercy and compassion.[6] Four centuries after Urakagina, Urnammu (2112–2095 B.C.), king of Sumer and Akkad, claimed to have established equity and justice in the land ". . . in accordance with the true word of [the god] Utu."[7] And Lipit-Ishtar, a later Sumerian (or Babylonian) king, who ruled early in the second millennium (1934–1924 B.C.), had himself described as the wise shepherd, chosen ". . . to establish justice in the land . . . [and to cause] righteousness and truth to shine forth."[8] The implications of much of this are decidedly ethical, not legal, and the ethical imperative seems to pass from god to king. In sharp contrast are the specific requirements of the law codes that follow them. It is of more than passing interest that the first legal statement of the principle of monetary compensation for injury is in the Code of Urnammu. Statute 15, for example, reads: "If a man . . . cut off the foot of [another man . . .] he shall pay ten shekels of silver." Other statutes set amounts to be paid for rape, divorce, adultery, and false accusation, as well as for various types of bodily injury,[9] but of ethical implication there is none, unless one perceives ethical stirrings in the transition from socially acceptable revenge killings for wrong or injury to orderly compensation supervised by the state.

A later code, that of Eshnunna (Bilalama), probably promulgated between 2000 and 1800 B.C., has no prologue but sets amounts of money to be paid for many sorts of bodily injury and damage to property. It also contains a statute concerning the ox that habitually gores which, like the similar statute of later date in Exodus (21:28–29), requires that if the ox kill a man the ox be stoned to death and its owner be fined (in the biblical version, the owner of the ox may also be put to death).[10]

The most famous of the cuneiform codes was promulgated by Hammurabi (1792–1750 B.C.) of the first Babylonian Dynasty.[11] In the present setting it has special significance, since among its 282 statutes are nine that relate to services of healers of some sort. Statutes 215–223 are as follows:

215. If a surgeon has made a deep incision in the body of a free man with a lancet of bronze and saves the man's life or has opened the caruncle in the eye of a man with a lancet of bronze and saves his eye, he shall take 10 shekels of silver.

216. If the patient is a villein, he shall take five shekels of silver.

217. If the patient is the slave of a free man, the master of the slave shall give two shekels of silver to the surgeon.

218. If the surgeon has made a deep incision in the body of a free man with a lancet of bronze and causes the man's death or has opened the caruncle in the eye of a man and so destroys the man's eye, they shall cut off his fore-hand.

219. If the surgeon has made a deep incision in the body of a villein's slave with a lancet of bronze and causes his death, he shall replace slave for slave.

220. If he has opened his caruncle with a lancet of bronze and destroys his eye, he shall pay half his price in silver.

221. If a surgeon mends the broken bone of a free man or heals a diseased muscle, the injured person shall give the physician five shekels of silver.

222. If he is a villein, he shall give three shekels of silver.

223. If he is the slave of a free man, he shall give the surgeon two shekels of silver.[12]

All nine statutes are either legal provisions for penalty to be inflicted on the healer in case of unsatisfactory therapeutic result or death (218–220), or laws governing the fees to be received for certain services (215–217, 221–223).

It is often said that statutes 218–220 are the earliest malpractice laws yet discovered. But neither they nor the statutes regulating fees possess discernible ethical implications, and it is incorrect to refer to the laws of Hammurabi as "the first recorded code of medical ethics."[13] Indeed, the only ethical content to be found in the laws of Hammurabi is, as usual in cuneiform law, in the prologue and epilogue. In the prologue, Hammurabi says that Marduk, Babylon's god in chief, commanded him to "set forth truth and justice throughout the land." In the epilogue, he says that the great gods have called him as the guardian of the people, "that the strong may not oppress the weak . . . to give justice to the orphan and the widow . . . [and] to give justice to the oppressed."[14]

We have no way of knowing how these premonitions of ethical thought came to the Sumerians or how widely accepted they were. According to Samuel Noah Kramer's reading of the record, the Sumerians cherished goodness, truth, justice, freedom, mercy, and compassion, among other virtues. Certain of their deities, a goddess called Nanshe in particular, sponsored ethical conduct and condemned transgres-

Hammurabi receiving the law from the god Marduk. From the diorite stele on which the laws of Hammurabi were engraved, now in the Louvre, Paris. Eighteenth century B.C. COURTESY OF GIRAUDON, PARIS/ART RESOURCE, INC., NEW YORK.

sors.[15] But to see in Sumerian or Babylonian legal documents suggestions of ethical thought as it applies to the medical profession can in no way be justified.

The meanings, in context, of the two words for healer used

in the laws of Hammurabi (translated as *surgeon*) are debatable. G. R. Driver and John C. Miles say that one of the words refers to a seer, a hydromancer, and the other to a person skilled in the preparation and use of medicines.[16] More recently, Edith K. Ritter has looked into the "two-valued system of healing" of the Babylonians and assigns distinct meanings to the two words customarily employed. She identifies a priestly healer who practiced magic, on the one hand, and a secular healer who employed more direct methods, on the other. The practitioner of magic derived his authority from the gods, and used incantations and various objects of special significance in ritual. "He is the man of tradition . . . of rote and of learning, the contemplative man of the world in a wide world." The magician did not touch the patient, but left that to the healer, who prepared and administered drugs, bathed and massaged the patient, and performed other services for him.[17] In some instances, the two healers seem to have worked cooperatively but, in Morris Jastrow's view, the magician-healer was held in greater esteem and awe than the secular healer. He may, in fact, have been above the law, while the manual practitioner, whose role was plainly secular, was subject like most others to legal penalty if he were responsible for certain types of injury.[18]

It is somewhat startling to find legal statutes promulgated long before the Greeks, and considerably before Moses's reception of the Decalogue, that required healers to pay compensation (or to lose the right hand) if their professional results were unsatisfactory. Sumerian civilization and its numerous innovations are collectively an astonishing phenomenon that seems to burst with great suddenness on the history of mankind. The appearance is a deceptive one, since the civilization had been under development for several millennia before the written record begins to reveal it to us. It contains many themes that seem thoroughly familiar to us; so familiar, in fact, that we may credit them with more sophisticated development than the record warrants. The transition from blood revenge to the principle of monetary compensation was undeniably a considerable sociolegal achievement; yet more impressive was the emergence of a system of ethics for rulers, obliging them to use power and authority not merely to further justice in the legal sense, but also to reach for the morally sublime. The theme had as yet nothing to do with medicine. The concept and theory of profession, embodying the expectation of ethical behavior on the part of the professional, were still to come.

The Pre-Exilic Prophets. A thousand years or so after Hammurabi, the concept of a ruler's ethic took a massive leap forward when certain inspired men began to warn the rulers of Israel and Judah of impending disaster because of their ungodly behavior. In the interim, the legal concept of compensation for injury was considerably advanced by the Assyrians and the Hittites, whose law was far from primitive, even though there was heavy accent on the law of talion[19] (eye for eye, tooth for tooth, etc.). Assyrian law mentions the physician once, but only tangentially.[20] Hittite law makes a person who has caused injury to another person liable for the physician's fee, but otherwise shows no concern for healers or healing.[21] There is, however, no evidence that either Assyrian or Hittite law was thought to be god-given, and neither corpus contains the ethical admonition of god to ruler so characteristic of Sumerian and early Babylonian prologues to legal codes.

The admonition is taken up with magnificent use of speech and imagery by Israel's pre-exilic prophets. The phenomenon of the pre-exilic prophets,[22] which began in the eighth

century B.C., is not easily explained. James H. Breasted, the
most enthusiastic of twentieth-century Egyptologists, insists
that "in morals, in religion, and in social thinking in general
. . . the Hebrews built their life on Egyptian foundations."[23] His contention, however, is difficult to support on
the basis of the Egyptian sources he cites.[24]

It was Amos, the first of the so-called literary prophets, who
ushered in the relatively brief era of the pre-exilic prophets.
Their purpose, as conduits of God's word, was to restore Israel and Judah to the straight and narrow path. They made
it clear from the beginning that they were not seers who went
into ecstatic trances in order to predict the future or diviners
who provided readings for anyone who could pay their fees.
Amos specifically denied that he was a professional prophet
(7:14); his mission was to receive and transmit the Lord's word.
Jeremiah made the distinction even clearer: let the prophet of
dreams and trances prophesy in terms of those dreams and
trances, but let him who is called to speak the Lord's word
speak it faithfully. Concluding the passage, Jeremiah asks:
"What is the chaff to the wheat?" (23:28), leaving little doubt
as to what, in his mind, was chaff and what was wheat.

The specific and extraordinary nature of the pre-exilic (also
called classical) prophets, has been explained by Abraham J.
Heschel, who deals at length with the complex relationship
in the ancient world between god, king, prophet, and law.[25]
Suffice it for present purposes to say that Israel, staunchly
rejecting the Egyptian tradition, neither deified her kings nor
placed them above the law. Nor were the classical prophets
the king's hirelings: on the contrary, the prophets were fear-
less and independent proponents of justice and righteousness.

Amos sounded the theme in one of the Old Testament's
most majestic and moving passages:

> Yea though ye offer me burnt-
> offerings and your meal-offerings
> I will not accept them . . .
> Take thou away from me the noise
> of thy songs;
> And let me not hear the melody
> of thy psalteries.
> *But let justice well up as waters*
> *And righteousness as a mighty*
> *stream.* [26]
>
> [Amos 5:23–24]

The same theme, always recognizing a distinction between justice and righteousness, is sounded again and again, directly and indirectly by most of the prophets that followed Amos. Jeremiah, prophesizing that Israel and Judah might enter on peace and prosperity if they would reform, said: "In those days and at that time, Will I cause the Branch of Righteousness to grow up into David: and he shall execute judgment and righteousness in the land." (Jeremiah 33:15). Isaiah I speaks of kings reigning in righteousness and princes ruling in judgment (32:1), and says the Lord of hosts shall be exalted in judgment; God that is holy shall be sanctified in righteousness (5:15). And he shall dwell on high who ". . . walketh righteously, and speaketh uprightly; he that despiseth the gain of oppressions, that shaketh his hands from holding of bribes. . . ." (33:16)

The marvel of the message transmitted by the pre-exilic prophets (especially Amos, Jeremiah, and Isaiah) is the power and the clarity of the ethical message: justice there must be but it is not, of and by itself, enough—there must also be righteousness. Heschel is explicit on the point: "Righteousness goes beyond justice. Justice is strict and exact, giving each person his due. Righteousness implies benevolence, kindness, generosity. . . . Justice may be legal; righteousness is

associated with a burning compassion for the oppressed. . . .[27]
Justice is administered by mortal men. Hence the message of
the prophets is usually directed at the rulers and the high and
mighty of Israel and Judah. But righteousness to the Hebrew
was of God.[28] Micah's solemn reminder is relevant: ". . . what
doth the Lord require of thee but to do justly and to love
mercy and to walk humbly with thy God?" (6:8) Just conduct must thus not stand alone; compassion and humility before God, both aspects of righteousness, are no less essential.[29]

The ethical sense of justice and righteousness in the books
of the prophets can hardly remain at issue.[30] The relationship
does not change if one views ethics, as do many modern philosophers, as an entity separate from religion. Considering the
philosophic and religious origins of the West in their entirety, even in our own time one separates the two somewhat
at one's peril: the word *righteousness* still has vague religious
connotations. But the equivalent words *morality* and *ethical-
ity*, referring as they do to something above and beyond mere
legality, have in modern usage little direct reference to religion.

To the pre-exilic prophets, however, such separation would
not only have been impossible: the suggestion would have been
incomprehensible. The point is that in a historical sense the
pre-exilic prophets take us to bedrock. They, for the first time,
bring us face to face with the grandeur and spaciousness of
the essence of ethical thought: to observe the law but also to
reach, of one's own volition, beyond it in the service of humanity. A lineal descendant is the New Testament concept
that "Unto whomsoever much is given, of him much shall be
required." (Luke 12:48)

It was an admonition that was directed at all men, Hebrew
and Gentile.[31] There is, however, evidence that in later cen-

turies the prophets' ethical imperative was redirected at priests and religious leaders. Still later, members of the medical profession ". . . shared common norms of professional conduct [with rabbis and judges] in several respects and enjoyed a similar status in the community."[32] The inference came to be that all three, as professionals, must go beyond the mere fulfillment of professional duty, the guiding principle being the ethical concept that righteousness goes beyond justice.

In that vast record of Jewish law and thought, the Babylonian Talmud, one finds the ethical imperative of the pre-exilic prophets taken up and tranlated vividly into the conditions of everyday life as they existed for several centuries before and after the beginning of the Christian era. When, for example, Rabbi Johanan says in *Baba Mezia* that Jerusalem was destroyed because its rulers ". . . based their judgments [strictly] upon Biblical law and did not go beyond the law," he is faithfully echoing Amos.[33] So also is Rab, when he instructs a plaintiff to go beyond the law, "that thou mayest walk in the way of good men."[34]

The position of the physician in Jewish society evolved, over the centuries, from one of no great significance to one of considerable respectability. In the early part of their history, the unshakable belief of the Jews in one all-powerful God led naturally to the view that only God could cure disease. Human beings who claimed to be healers were interlopers (and often non-Jews) who, at best, were no more than God's helpers.[35] But by the beginning of the Talmudic period (roughly 200 B.C. to A.D. 600), the medical calling had risen a notch or two, if one may judge from a reference to physicians in the apocryphal book Ecclesiasticus (probably written in the second century B.C.): "Cultivate the physician in accordance with the need of him, for him also hath God ordained. It is from God that the physician getteth wisdom, and from the king he receiveth gifts. The skill of the physician lifteth up his head, and he may stand before nobles."[36] (38:1–3) Still later, the physician and the medical profession came to be honored in Jewish society, so much so that penalties for inadequate performance by practitioners were seldom applied.[37] In regulations dating from the fourth century A.D. designed specifically to govern the performance of physicians, the general assumption seems to be that unless there was guile or evil intent on the part of the physician, fatal therapeutic results did not make him liable. A related medieval interpretation quoted by Immanuel Jakobovits says simply that if the physician had done his best, fatal issue was because "the Creator desired the patient's death."[38] The physician is liable for damages only in the case of injuries resulting from departure from ". . . the proper bounds within which the operation should have been confined."[39] But if a physician, however skillful, can be shown to have deliberately inflicted nonfatal injury, he is liable for damages or penalty.

The development by the Talmudists of a body of law governing negligence (on the part of anyone, physician or layman) was an astonishingly sophisticated achievement, the primary design of which seems to have been to mitigate the dire provisions of the law of talion. Set out in the Babylonian Talmud under the generic title *Nezikin* (from the Hebrew root meaning to damage or injure), the sense of its principal theme is the duty to take care if one has in one's control something that is ". . . in the habit of doing damage," or that may, if misapplied, do injury.[40] And negligence (*peshiah*) in Talmudic law ". . . includes every kind of breach of duty, whether recklessness, gross carelessness, or ordinary negligence."[41] Although Talmudic law under the heading *Nezikin* includes some acts that in contemporary law are considered crimes, the penalties preferred were in the form of compensation paid to the injured party, rather than punishment imposed by the state. Rabbis and judges of the Talmudic period are said to have preferred, in any case, to "direct men's minds to the moral, rather than to the legal, quality of their acts."[42] Long after the Talmudic period Maimonides, in his Mishneh Torah, which includes a book on wrongs (or torts as in Anglo-American common law), quoted Ezekiel (33:11) in support of the same emphasis:[43] "I have no pleasure in the death of the wicked but [rather] that the wicked turn from his way and live."

The Hebraic tradition as it pertains to both ethics and law, and as begun by Amos in the eighth century b.c., is thus one that covers a very long span of time and that proceeded parallel to other strivings of the same general category in the ancient world. For present purposes it is significant to note that the northern kingdom (Israel) disappeared soon after Homer sang his epics, and that the archaic age of Greece (roughly 800–500 b.c.) was drawing to a close about the time Jewish exiles were returning, with Cyrus's blessing, from Babylon to Jerusalem. The *Iliad* and the *Odyssey* had, by this time, probably been committed to writing, as had much of the Old Testament, including the books of the pre-exilic prophets. But the Talmud was not yet.

Nor had the Golden Age of Greece begun. That critically important period in the life of the West dates, by convention, from the Greek victories over the Persians at Marathon, Platae, and Mycale (490–479 b.c.). The Hebraic and the Greek cultural phenomena, each vast in its own scope, proceeded independently for several centuries; when contact was finally established, the result was mostly conflict. Much of Rome's culture, with the important exception of its legal system in its fully developed form, was imported from Greece.

2 · The Greeks: Hippocratic Medicine and Ethics

Karl Jaspers identifies what he calls the axial period of world history ". . . in the spiritual process that occurred between 800 and 200 B.C. It is there that we meet the most deepcut dividing line in history. Man, as we know him today, came into being."[1] In this connection, Jaspers specifies the spiritual process: that composite of human hopes and feelings that encompasses religion, what we today call philosophy and ethics, and, to a lesser extent, law. In these areas, the seminal achievements that occurred within the time limits he set are the Hebraic and the Greek.

The Hebraic cultural achievement of the eighth and seventh centuries B.C. has tended to be overshadowed by Greek accomplishments during the Golden Age of Greece, which fell mostly in the fifth century B.C. They were, as Cyrus H. Gordon points out, parallel but independent developments.[2] Greeks are mentioned in at least three Old Testament books, but the references are casual or negative in each instance. There is no suggestion of transmission of religious precept or philosophic thought from Hebrew to Greek during the period specified by Jaspers.[3]

The Greek cultural achievements that have been so instru-
mental in shaping Western civilization are usually taken to have
begun with Homer's epics, the consensus being that he lived
during the late ninth or early eighth century B.C. The action
in both epics took place, however, much earlier, reaching back
to Mycenean times.[4] Archaeologic evidence fixes the fall of
the Troy of the *Iliad*, actually the seventh city built on the
site, at about the middle of the thirteenth century B.C., i.e.,
1250 B.C. or slightly later.[5] As for Homer himself, Herodotus tells us that the great epic poet's time was "not more than
four hundred years before my own."[6] Herodutus' own birth
year may be reasonably fixed at 484 B.C., thus indicating the
first quarter of the ninth century B.C. as a time when Homer
was alive.

Homer was a product of what is today usually referred to
as the Archaic Age of Greece (circa 800–500 B.C.). The period probably deserves a more positive and impressive designation: it saw the emergence of Greek democracy[7] as well
as revolutionary change in the country's economy from
something like the palace economy described by Homer to a
vigorous economy based on a free market that reached far and
wide in the Mediterranean basin.[8] Greek philosophy also had
its beginning during the Archaic Age, especially in Ionia
(western Turkey) and southern Italy. But classical Greek
philosophy and ethics as we ordinarily view them[9] are mainly
products of the Golden Age.[10]

Relevant Currents of Greek Political Thought. In Homer's time,
Greece was composed of a series of self-contained communities, each ruled by a king or an aristocracy or a combination
of the two. Remnants of division into tribes (three Doric, four
Ionian) still persisted and were still to be seen in the fifth
century, when Athens adopted a democratic form of govern-

ment. It all came about gradually, beginning (probably) with Solon's legislation about 594 B.C. and culminating with the actions of Ephialtes and Pericles in 462 B.C., which deprived the aristocracy of the remnants of special privileges.[11] The high point of Greek democracy may be taken as the much-quoted funeral oration delivered by Pericles in 431 B.C., during Socrates' lifetime and a few years before Plato was born.[12] Pericles described Athens' government as a democracy, "in the hands not of the few but of the many," and went on to say that all were equal before the law, and that Athenians, unlike those whom the Greeks haughtily labelled *hoi barbaroi*, respected not only those laws "which are ordained for the succor of the oppressed," but also those which "though unwritten, bring upon the transgressor a disgrace which all men recognize."

Pericles thus attributed to Athenians a sense of the legal and an appreciation of the supralegal, a distinction that is suggestive of that drawn so persistently by the pre-exilic prophets between justice and righteousness (or legality and morality). But Pericles' political views were for the most part opposed to those advocated by Plato and, later, by Aristotle; both seem to have rejected egalitarianism in any form, and both accepted slavery as a matter of course.[13] Such views, along with the glorification of Greece's tribal past, brought Werner Fite to the conclusion that ". . . Plato deliberately turned his back . . . upon what is still regarded as the highest point in Greek civilization . . . and embraced the barbarism of Sparta."[14] More recently, Karl Popper developed a similar point of view concerning Plato's (and Aristotle's) political views. Popper commented extensively on Plato's retreat to ". . . idealized tribal progenitors and heroes" as an antidote to social change and as the basis for suppressing all innovation in education, legislation, and religion.[15]

The Myths and Cult of Asklepius. The Greek medical or healing tradition, like Plato's social and political views, reaches back to its tribal past, the influence of which was still powerful even as late as Pericles' day. Athens, in Ernest Barker's view, was not a city-state, but a tribal-state; the state "in Athens, Sparta, and Greece generally was a living tribe and a personal order of man . . . conscious of its unity and [incorporating] its consciousness in common and special cult of one of the great deities."[16] As the Archaic Age waned, the tribal-state ultimately became the city-state, but the legacies of the former were still visible, sometimes looming large, as indeed, they did in Plato's mind. They are also to an extent visible in the emergence of Greek medicine, the traditional lineage of which runs from Apollo (one of the Olympian twelve) to Asklepius (his son by a mortal princess) to Hippocrates who, in a symbolic sense, seems to have counted himself a lineal descendant of Asklepius; so did Aristotle.[17] Ancient and not-so-ancient authors offered specific genealogies that showed Hippocrates to be the lineal descendant of Asklepius.[18]

Who Asklepius really was and what he represented in archaic and classical Greek society are items that remain unclear. The study by Emma and Ludwig Edelstein, in which are cited many ancient authors who mention Asklepius, leaves unsolved several key questions, especially those that concern Asklepius and his family cult in the Archaic Age.[19]

The earliest mention of Asklepius is in the *Iliad*, where Homer describes him as "the great healer" and the father of Podaleirus, the physician learned in the use of drugs, and of Machaon, the battlefield surgeon.[20] The rise of the Asklepian myth and the spread of the Asklepian priestly healing cult were both post-Homeric phenomena. The several versions of the myth assign the beginnings to Thessaly, and are narrated by several classical authors, including Pindar, Pausanias, and Appollodorus. All agree that Apollo, possibly with the help of Cheiron the Centaur, taught the art of healing to his son.[21]

However this may have been, a powerful priestly cult of healers, claiming tribal relationship to Asklepius, grew up in Greece and spread thence through the ancient world. A temple, built at Epidaurus about 430 B.C., came to be the model for Asklepian centers as they were established elsewhere in the ancient world.[22] Asklepian centers were set up in Athens in 420 B.C., at Delphi about 400 B.C., at Pergamum about the same time, and—most significantly—not before about 250 B.C. at Kos, the legendary home of Hippocrates.[23]

During the Archaic Age the Asklepian priestly cult may have maintained a monopoly of healing. It seems to have considered itself a family cult in the Greek tradition, whereby the secrets of craft or cult were transmitted from father to son, and to others only by swearing them in as adopted family members. Many ancient authors, including Galen, support some such view.[24] The Edelsteins agree that medicine as a craft ". . . slipped out of the hands of the sons of Asklepius" and that they tried to maintain the tradition of family cult or craft by use of adoption. But ultimately, the Asklepian modifier came to be used generically, referring to all those who practiced medicine.[25] Hippocrates, who came in time to be called "The Great" to distinguish him from his grandfather who bore the same name, was in this sense probably an Asklepian. But there is no evidence that he was himself a priest or that he used Asklepian ritual in treating patients. Nor can it be maintained that the Hippocratic Corpus was in whole or in part based on observations made and recorded in Asklepian temples.[26] Very noteworthy in this connection is that Asklepius' name appears only once in the entire Hippocratic Corpus, and that is in the *Oath*.

Hippocratic Science and Ethics. The collection of Greek works on medical topics known to us as the Hippocratic Corpus is of uncertain date and authorship, and there is no final agreement among scholars as to which works belong in the Corpus and which do not. It is generally accepted that collections of works attributed to Hippocrates were assembled by scholars at the Alexandrian Library[27] in the second century B.C., that most were written between 430 and 350 B.C., and that they may originally have been brought together in the library of a school.[28]

The themes that are especially important in justifying the exalted position of the Hippocratics in the history of Western medicine appear most prominently in two of the nearly seventy titles W. H. S. Jones includes in the Hippocratic Corpus. In *The Sacred Disease (On Epilepsy)* the tradition that the gods cause disease is summarily rejected; in *Ancient Medicine*, the philosophers' hypothetical speculations are rejected in favor of the use of empirical observation in arriving at logical conclusions in medical matters.[29] But "the Hippocratic collection is a medley, with no inner bond of union except that all the works are written in the Ionic dialect and are connected more or less closely with medicine or one of its allied sciences. There are the widest possible divergences of style, and the sharpest possible contradictions in doctrine."[30] Why, then, did the Hippocratic Corpus in one form or another survive so long and, during most of its long life span, exert such a powerful effect on so many generations of medical men? The answer must be that, despite the disorderliness of thought and style in the Corpus, it embodied ". . . a consistent doctrine of theory and practice, free from both superstitions and philosophy, and setting forth rational empiricism of a strictly scientific character."[31]

But what of so-called Hippocratic ethics and the *Oath* attributed to Hippocrates? The *Oath* (and the *Law*), according to Jones, contain ". . . those noble rules, loyal obedience to which has raised the calling of the physician to be the highest of all the professions."[32] Scrutiny of the precise contents of the *Oath*, especially in the light of certain of Edelstein's findings (see below), suggest that Jones's first description ("sharpest possible contradictions in doctrine") is more accurate than the second.

Mention of an oath occurs very early in the works of ancient authors that relate to the Hippocratics. Erotian (c. A.D. 50) seems to have been the first. He lists *Oath, Law, Art,* and *Ancient Medicine* in one grouping but says nothing about the content of the *Oath*.[33] Scribonius Largus, a Roman author writing in the first century A.D., also mentions the *Oath* and describes some of its content; enough, in fact, to reinforce the belief that the currently accepted version is substantially the same as it was in Scribonius' time.[34] But Galen (A.D. 150–190) made no mention of *Oath, Law, Art,* or *Ancient Medicine*.[35] This, to Francis Adams, was a serious barrier to acceptance of any of the four.[36] Erotian, however, listed all of the works in question and, while the *Oath* is not included in the earliest extant manuscript of Hippocratic works (tenth century), it appears in manuscripts of the eleventh and twelfth centuries.[37] E. Littré, the great French scholar of the early nineteenth century, accepted *Oath* as genuine and says that without a doubt an Asklepian wrote it.[38] Adams also accepted it, largely on the authority of Erotian,[39] and so on various grounds, have more recent authors including Jones, Karl Deichgräber,[40] and Edelstein.

The authorship of the *Oath*, Littré notwithstanding, cannot be established. Jones would like to believe that at least the nucleus of the *Oath* goes back to Hippocrates himself and that "nobody else is more likely to have framed such a fine guide to medical morality."[41] Saras Nittis accepts as probable that the *Oath* was written by Hippocrates in Athens be-

OATH

I swear by Apollo Physician and Asclepius and Hygieia and Panaceia and all the gods and goddesses, making them my witnesses, that I will fulfil according to my ability and judgment this oath and this covenant:

To hold him who has taught me this art as equal to my parents and to live my life in partnership with him, and if he is in need of money to give him a share of mine, and to regard his offspring as equal to my brothers in male lineage and to teach them this art—if they desire to learn it—without fee and covenant; to give a share of precepts and oral instruction and all the other learning to my sons and to the sons of him who has instructed me and to pupils who have signed the covenant and have taken an oath according to the medical law, but to no one else.

I will apply dietetic measures for the benefit of the sick according to my ability and judgment; I will keep them from harm and injustice.

I will neither give a deadly drug to anybody if asked for it, nor will I make a suggestion to this effect. Similarly I will not give to a woman an abortive remedy. In purity and holiness I will guard my life and my art.

I will not use the knife, not even on sufferers from stone, but will withdraw in favor of such men as are engaged in this work.

Whatever houses I may visit, I will come for the benefit of the sick, remaining free of all intentional injustice, of all mischief and in particular of sexual relations with both female and male persons, be they free or slaves.

What I may see or hear in the course of the treatment or even outside of the treatment in regard to the life of men, which on no account one must spread abroad, I will keep to myself holding such things shameful to be spoken about.

If I fulfil this oath and do not violate it, may it be granted to me to enjoy life and art, being honored with fame among all men for all time to come; if I transgress it and swear falsely, may the opposite of all this be my lot.

The Oath *attributed to Hippocrates, pagan version, as translated by Ludwig Edelstein. Ludwig Edelstein, "The Hippocratic Oath. Text, Translation, and Interpretation." Supplement No. 1. Bull. Hist. Med. (1943), p. 3.*

tween March and October of 421 B.C.[42] Both views can only be classed as fanciful. Most nineteenth-century authorities and many of those writing in the first half of the twentieth century, with the exception of Edelstein, believed that the model on which the *Oath* was based was of Asklepian origin. Littré believed that it was written by a physician in the Hippocratic era and (as noted above) that the author was himself Asklepian. Charles Victor Daremberg thought that the basic formula of the *Oath* was Asklepian and that Hippocrates modified it to the form we now know.[43] Jones's views on the point are equivocal,[44] but Robert Fuchs says flatly that the *Oath* is an *Asklepiadenstatut*, that it is one of the oldest items in the Corpus, and that it originated on Kos.[45] George Thomson agrees in principle.[46]

Edelstein turned his attention to the origin and meaning of the *Oath* in 1943 and radically altered the views that to that time had prevailed. By far his most important contribution was to show that certain prohibitions in the *Oath* were Pythagorean dogma and not, in any sense, Hippocratic.[47] Edelstein's reference was to the prohibitions in the *Oath* of deadly drugs (almost certainly at the request of an individual with suicidal intent), agents that produce abortion, and surgical procedures that require use of the knife. These procedures were forbidden in fifth-century Greece only by the Pythagoreans, a cult with a special interest in health and medicine.[48] Edelstein thus provided an explanation for what has for centuries been a very puzzling portion of the *Oath*, by which no Greek physician could have been bound unless he was a member of the Pythagorean cult. Emphasis on diet was also a feature of Pythagorean belief and so may have been the injunction to keep patients from mischief and injustice, especially that which is self-inflicted through improper diet or regimen. The proscription of sexual relations with "both male and female persons" is in keeping with the Pythagorean condemnation of sexual activity in general, except where procreation is the specific purpose.[49]

As for the covenant in the *Oath* whereby the aspirant swears to regard his teacher as his father, to transmit his learning to his own children and to his teacher's, and to "pupils who have signed the covenant and have taken an oath," Edelstein says simply that it ". . . must be influenced by Pythagorean philosophy."[50] In this connection Diodorus Siculus says that "Pythagoras . . . commanded his pupils rarely to take an oath, and, when they did swear to an oath, to abide by it under any circumstances,"[51] but gives no details as to the content of the oath. Finally, Edelstein maintains that swearing by Apollo and Asklepius was standard form for all medical oaths, and that the presence of Asklepius' name in the opening lines of the *Oath* implies nothing with regard to the Asklepian medical-family guild.[52]

On these several grounds, Edelstein says that the *Oath*, in spirit and in letter, in form and content, ". . . is a Pythagorean manifesto. . . . All indications point to the conclusion that the *Oath* is a Pythagorean document."[53] But he stops short of removing Hippocrates' name from the title: in his study the *Oath* is still the Hippocratic—not the Pythagorean—Oath. He thus denies, on questionable grounds, the older contention that the *Oath* as we know it may be an adaptation for Pythagorean purposes of a much older Asklepian instrument devised to permit the acceptance of outsiders into the Asklepian "family."

None of this, however, seriously impairs Edelstein's conclusion ". . . that the Hippocratic *Oath* is . . . not [an] expression of an absolute standard of medical conduct."[54] Nor does such evidence as is available clearly deny the earlier, largely nineteenth-century view that the predecessor of the

Oath was an Asklepian instrument for processing non-Asklepian applicants and is thus a remnant, in a significant sense, of Greece's tribal past.

Of much greater importance than any of these specialized debates is the fact, first made clear by Edelstein, that the *Oath* of Hippocrates is not, and cannot ever have been, a guide to ethical conduct for the physician (unless, in the ancient world, he were also Pythagorean). To the modern, virtually none of the *Oath's* content seems to possess genuinely ethical reference unless the good being sought is that of the Art *(techné)*— Asklepian, Hippocratic, or Pythagorean. Part of the problem is that the ancient Greeks had no concept of profession in the modern sense. "The Greeks . . . recognized no distinction between a craft or 'trade' and a 'profession'."[55] Physicians, like prophets, sculptors, and poet-singers were craftsmen. At some time each had its guild, members of which were looked on symbolically as descendants of a divine, or quasi-divine founder, "the eponymous ancestor."[56]

Whatever views one may hold concerning the origins of the *Oath* attributed to Hippocrates, it cannot be looked on as a great source of medical ethics, its chief purpose having been, as Edelstein has shown, much more mundane and pragmatic. In his words, "the Hippocratic physician is a craftsman," and the *Oath* in no way alters his status.[57] With reference to the attitude of the Greek physician toward his patient, ". . . which is so highly praised in today's discussions," Edelstein reminds us that it must be considered in context and that it ". . . was conditioned by the circumstances of ancient medicine. . . ."[58]

Looked at in this light, the *Oath* in our own time becomes little more than an interesting antique, preserved and revered for two millennia by amiable custom, itself dependent to some extent on medicine's tradition of authority. As for attitudes of the Hippocratics that reach from the merely legal to the moral sphere, we learn a good deal more from the other so-called deontologic writings of the Hippocratics[59] than from the *Oath*.

Greek Law and the Medical Craft. Much of the confusion about the meaning of the *Oath* attributed to Hippocrates can thus be attributed to the tendency of physicians' groups in later centuries to avulse it from its classical Greek context. The Greeks failed to evolve a full-fledged code of professional ethics and, in fact, got only part way to evolving a concept and theory of profession.

It remains to inquire what Greek law had to say about the obligations of practitioners of the many crafts to their clients. Unlike the Romans, the Greeks left no great bodies of legal writing, nor did they evolve a body of law that was applicable throughout the Greek world. Each city-state had its own, although certain legal principles were probably common to most. The fatal weakness of the city-states was, however, their inability to find common cause for very long in any sphere. They proved to be a political form that very quickly ran its course.

The Homeric epics give very little insight into the law of the Mycenean period or the Greek Dark Ages. The principle that male might makes right, and a theme of brutality of the goriest sort, run consistently through the *Iliad* and, to a lesser extent, through the *Odyssey*. References to law are few and usually refer to the primitive duty to avenge homicide, and certain other offenses, by murdering the wrongdoer. Odysseus was acting under customary law against usurpation and adultery when he and his son slaughtered Penelope's suitors. Customary law then required the families of the deceased suitors to murder Odysseus in turn, and they would doubtless have done so had not Athena conveniently intervened. Similarly, Agamemnon's murder by Aegisthus was avenged as a matter of course by Orestes, helped by Athena. In both epics, such violence is fully acceptable to, and indeed expected by, both men and gods.[60]

There is a description in the *Iliad* of a trial scene that was probably drawn from Homer's time, rather than from the much earlier Mycenean period. In the scene,[61] which is engraved on Achilles' shield, a defendant on trial claims that he has paid the blood-price of a man he killed, accidentally or otherwise; the plaintiff says he has received nothing. Both seek settlement by arbitration. The town elders in the scene sit in some sort of judicial capacity and the populace, restrained by heralds, also delivers judgment. Legal historians still debate the meaning of the scene, some seeing in it the origin of trial by jury.[62] For present purposes its importance is the evidence it provides that by Homer's time an established and orderly legal method for settling differences between individuals was in process of replacing the more primitive blood-feud.

Very little Greek law has come down to us in writing, although Strabo, writing shortly before the beginning of the Christian era, says that the first written laws in Greece were compiled by the Locrians, probably in the seventh century B.C. Zaleneas, who compiled them, says Strabo, based them on Cretan, Laconian, and Areopagite customary law.[63] Other western Greek colonies are said to have followed suit; Dracon's famous laws for Athens are dated by tradition to about 621 B.C. None of these laws has come down to us in written form, but Dracon's laws have survived by evil reputation transmitted mostly by Plutarch;[64] hence our adjective draconian. The most important of Dracon's laws, that dealing with homicide, has come down to us through a republication on a marble stele, dated about 409–408 B.C.[65] It is of special pertinence since, when Solon was called on to revise Dracon's laws (circa 594–593 B.C.), he is said by no less an authority than Aristotle to have disposed of all of them except that dealing with homicide.[66] Its chief purpose seems to have been to prevent the revenge killing by surviving relatives of one guilty of involuntary homicide. The basic penalty provided by Dracon in such cases was exile, but the nearest relatives could, by unanimous vote, pardon the accidental killer altogether. It seems clear, as affirmed by Douglas MacDowell, that Dracon's law of homicide was of major importance in that it provided Athenian authorities with judicial means of limiting revenge killings and provided guidelines for those required to render decisions. However, the relatives of the deceased, not the state, had to press charges.[67]

The oldest written law in Europe is the collection discovered between 1857 and 1884 at Gortyn, a village near Phaistos in southern Crete. All except one small portion of the collection (now in the Louvre) is still on display at Gortyn, the clay archive measuring about five by thirty feet and containing six hundred lines written in archaic Greek. The date of the collection is probably early sixth century (circa 600 B.C.). The content of the laws suggests that they are not a complete code but, rather, a collection of amendments to pre-existing law of which we have no record.[68] They deal mostly with family law, slavery, and matters having to do with the ownership of property, especially that transmitted by inheritance. But undoubtedly their most striking feature is the authority assigned to judicial bodies to regulate disputes between individuals and the substitution of compensation in money, in lieu of self-help and the blood feud, for wrongs that included rape and adultery. Acting on the earlier customary law of the Mycenean period, Odysseus, as we have seen, murdered his wife's suitors en masse. But had he lived under the

Column XI of the law code of Gortyn (Crete), the oldest known written law in Europe. The inscription employs an archaic Greek alphabet of eighteen letters and the boustrophedon *system: the first line is inscribed right-to-left, the second left-to-right, and the third right-to-left, and so on to the end. This excerpt deals with the legal rights of adoptive sons and adopters. From Ronald Willetts* The Law Code of Gortyn *(Berlin: Walter de Gruyter and Co., 1967).* COURTESY OF THE PUBLISHER.

laws of Gortyn, he would, at most, have been awarded money compensation by those of the wrongdoers who were, under the provisions of the law, proved to be guilty of rape or adultery. Under the circumstances, the wrongdoers would each have had to pay Odysseus one hundred staters, and if they failed to pay up within five days he would then, but only then, have been permitted to enslave or murder them at his whim.[69]

If he had seized any of the alleged wrongdoers prior to trial, he would have been fined and required by the court to release the captive within three days.

Greek law had thus moved a long way in the six centuries or so that separated the times of which Homer sang from those to which the laws of Gortyn pertained. Judging from the *Odyssey*, the fine for adultery was not unknown in the days of the epics, especially if the adulterer were a god. When Ares, god of war and father of Eros, was caught in flagrante delicto with Aphrodite by her lame husband Haephaestus, the other gods, tittering among themselves, judged that Ares owed Haephaestus "the fine of the adulterer."[70]

There is no mention in the laws of Gortyn of healers and therefore no suggestion of the position of physicians in the eyes of the law. There is, however, rather clear evidence that by about 450 B.C., physicians were accorded a unique position by legal custom, if not by statute. The evidence is in the form of three groups of four short speeches, each known as a tetralogy, said to have been composed as an academic exercise by an Athenian teacher of rhetoric during the classical period. Antiphon, the author, deals with homicide in several of his speeches; in the third tetralogy, an old man dies after having been in a fight with a young one. The young man pleads in his own defense that the old man's death was due to the incompetence of the physician called to treat the injured party and not to the blows he administered (in self-defense). The opposing side said that "even if his death was due to the physician, which it was not, the physician is not his murderer because the law absolves him from guilt."[71] The physician, competent or otherwise, intended the patient no harm and was not therefore subject to penalty.

The evidence provided by Antiphon's third tetralogy has been questioned by Darrell Amundsen, who maintains that classical Greek law held the physician accountable for incompetence and negligence. He dismisses Antiphon's statement of the law on the ground that it was merely a hypothetical teaching device.[72] Plato, however, bears out the view that is inherent in Antiphon's third tetralogy. In *The Laws*, his final opus, he says that if a physician unintentionally causes a patient's death in the course of treatment, he is not to suffer penalty.[73] If, however, he intentionally poisons a patient, even though the patient does not die, he is to be put to death. The physician must, Plato adds parenthetically, construct a full case history and must give no prescription until he has obtained the patient's understanding and consent.[74] The requirements, however, obtained only if the patient was a free man. If a slave, he could be tended by the physician's assistant, who owed the patient nothing by way of explanation or justification.

Aristotle takes much the same line vis-à-vis the position of the physician in Greek law. A physician himself and the son of a physician, Aristotle's statements about doctors are generally favorable. He says nothing to suggest that the legal principle set out by Antiphon and affirmed by Plato did not, in his time, still prevail. In *Politics*, he gives physicians credit for being honorable and impartial in their professional lives, ". . . whereas magistrates do many things from spite and partiality."[75] The men of law in Athens no doubt took issue, as do their twentieth-century counterparts, with Aristotle's uneven comparison of the two professions; he can have had no knowledge of the uses and misuses to which the peer-group prerogative would be put by professional guilds in later millennia. He thought, in fact, that physicians, not laymen, should judge physicians, and ". . . so ought men in general to be called to account by their peers."[76] He adds that the word doctor is used in three different senses: there are ordinary physicians, specialists, and the layman who has acquired a general knowledge of medicine. When these distinctions began to be recognized is not clear, but they leave little doubt that in Aristotle's time some sort of healing profession, distinct from the cult of Asklepius, existed. The Greek patient in Aristotle's time must therefore have had available a variety of providers of health services. But Greek law still had nothing to say about incompetence or negligence specifically on the part of the physician. The Greek physician *may* have recognized an ethical obligation to keep himself pure and to bring no discredit to his professional brotherhood, but his ethical obligation to his patient, ill-defined to say the least, came after his obligation to self and guild.

We should not, wrote J. C. Stobart in 1911, ". . . overrate the importance of that narrow strip of time which scholars select out of Greek history as the 'classical period'."[77] The classical period gave way to the Hellenistic which, in turn, was ultimately superseded by Roman conventions and language. But Hellenism was not entirely displaced, even with the fall of Rome, and important aspects of it lingered on in the world of Byzantium.

When Alexander the Great died in 323 B.C., his mentor and teacher Aristotle was driven from Athens by the accusation of impiety, the ancient version of the modern American quasilegal security risk. He lived on at Chalcis (now Khalkis) only a year, succumbing in 322 B.C. to a stomach ailment. Greek scholarship and language, far from dying, spread far afield, partly owing to the Greek diaspora, an intermittent process that lasted well past the beginning of the Christian era, and in important measure to the enlightened policies of the Alexandrian Museum and Library.

Rome, at first suspicious of things Greek, embraced Greek

culture with little reservation in the several centuries after the birth of Christ. The Roman genius for law and political organization, however, owed little to the Greeks. But by Rome's Silver Age, its grandest cultural period, its traditions had become a magnificent amalgam of the Greek and the Roman. The span from A.D. 96 to A.D. 180, encompassing the reigns of Nerva, Trajan, Hadrian, Antoninus Pius, and Marcus Aurelius, was a short and brilliant climactic interval within much longer spans, before and after, of gloomy and bloody human strivings and mostly self-inflicted disasters. Sentimental scholarly tradition and distortion (and even destruction of the historical record by religious zealots and others) have deprived us of an accurate account of Rome's greatest glory, a deficiency that is only now being gradually set right. Within the interval, but not earlier, concepts of profession, ethics, and law (and the always dynamic interface between ethics and law), as we know them today, began to take shape.

3 · Roman Influence and
the Dark Ages

Greece was taken over by the Romans in 146 B.C., but the reverence of the Romans for Greek cities and intellectual achievement made them reluctant to treat Greece as conquered territory. And although Corinth was destroyed as a warning, Athens remained the university city and intellectual capital of the ancient world until Justinian closed the city's schools of philosophy in A.D. 529. Although Rome's conservative upper classes were traditionally suspicious of Greek intellectual trends, Homer's epics were translated into Latin quite early (272 B.C.),[1] and the education of well-born Roman youths was almost exclusively in the hands of Greek tutors, usually slaves. As Horace put it: "Greece, the captive, made her savage victor captive and brought the arts into rustic Latium."[2]

Communication between Greece and Rome was probably lively even during the days of the kingdom (c. 735–510 B.C.) corresponding roughly to the Archaic Period of Greece (800–500 B.C.). Tradition has it that the Roman republic sent a delegation to Athens to study Solon's laws prior to drawing up its Twelve Tables in 450 B.C.[3] The Twelve Tables, although relatively primitive in structure and content, were the foundation stone on which Rome's stupendous legal structure was subsequently built. They have not come down to us intact, but relatively reliable reconstructions of them are available.[4]

Greek Medicine and Roman Law. Greek medicine came officially to Rome in 292 B.C. when, in the midst of a major epidemic, possibly bubonic plague, Roman authorities journeyed to Delphi to seek Apollo's help. The oracle instructed them to go to Epidaurus, where dwelt Asklepius, Apollo's son. There Asklepius, in the form of a snake, boarded the Roman ship and came with them to an island in the Tiber, where a shrine was constructed for him.[5] More credible is that over the next five centuries, many Greek physicians followed their eponymous father to Rome. According to Pliny the Elder, the first Greek physician to arrive was Archagathus, who came in 219 B.C. and who prospered despite the acquisition of an opprobrius nickname (Executioner).[6] Pliny also tells us that Cato considered all things Greek to be effete, corrupt, and un-Roman, but of all Greek institutions, Greek medicine and Greek doctors were to Cato the most reprehensible.[7]

Cato presumably represented the conservative views of Roman citizens who lived before the days of the empire and vast wealth. In their view, medical care was the responsibility of the pater familias and treatment was drawn from folklore, rather than from the rational system of the Hippocratics.

Roman law of the time suggests that doctors' services were occasionally sought despite Cato's counsel. The *lex Aquilia*, which dates from 286 B.C. or thereabouts, and which largely superseded Table VIII *(iniuriae)* of the Twelve Tables,[8] includes several references to physicians and medical care. For example: if a son loses an eye in an accident, the person responsible must compensate the son's father for the value of the son's service, lost because of the accident, and for the cost of medical treatment.[9] Legal action was allowed if a slave died from blows received, provided death was not due to the ignorance of the attending physician;[10] if a surgeon operated negligently on a slave or abandoned his patient, "he is deemed to be guilty of negligence."[11] At first glance, Roman law in this instance regarded slaves merely as property, and not as beings with legal rights of their own. Yet, as F. H. Lawson points out, Roman law came to regard slaves as both persons and things. Damage to slaves due to negligence came under the *lex Aquilia*, like damage to animals or inanimate property, but it was also personal injury and had, ultimately, to be regarded as such.[12] Roman law never seems to have developed rules providing penalty for the death of a freedman caused by the negligence of another person, either physician or layman, much less for nonfatal injury. The concept that fault (of omission or commission), or negligence, creates an obligation to pay compensation is of later date.[13]

In addition to physicians and surgeons, Roman law mentions midwives, who were judged guilty of murder if they administered fatal potions with their own hands.[14] But the *lex Aquilia* as contained in the Digest of Justinian (Book 9, Title 2) did not spell out a law of medical malpractice, as such. It contained the Roman law of *delicts*, which dealt primarily with "wrongful" damage to property but which also embraced a great deal that is included in the modern law of torts.[15] Roman law, where actions for damage unintentionally inflicted were concerned, gave doctors no special place, possibly because men of medicine in Roman society had for so long been Greek slaves. Most well-to-do Roman households included a *servus medicus*, many of whom were later freed,[16] and by Caesar's time Greek physicians were encouraged to immigrate to Rome as free citizens. Several later Roman rulers gave special rights and privileges to members of the medical calling.[17]

Nonetheless, the medical calling was never as acceptable in Roman aristocractic society as was law and, of course, politics. Most physicians were slaves, freedmen, or the descendants of freedmen, even late in the empire.[18] This may, in part, account for the fact that Rome produced no great medical innovators of her own. Celsus, an accomplished Roman author of the time of Tiberius (A.D. 14–37), was an encyclopedist who summarized other men's work but contributed no original work of his own. Galen (born A.D. 131, died A.D. 199) was a physician whose work has been called the summit of the Hippocratic edifice.[19] But he was born and reared a Greek, and was educated as a philosopher before turning to medicine.

Precursors of the Concept of Profession. What seems to have been a consistent deemphasis of the medical calling by the Romans cannot, per se, be taken as evidence of intellectual backwardness. In other fields, notably law, the Roman achievement was far superior to that of the Greeks. The Roman school of rhetoric normally and naturally led to the law,[20] and the ideal product of Roman higher education, according to Quintillian, was a lawyer (advocate) ". . who to extraordinary natural gifts has added a thorough mastery of all the fairest branches of knowledge, a man sent by heaven to be the blessing of mankind . . ." uniquely perfect in every detail and utterly noble in thought and speech alike.[21] Inherent are concepts that are suggestive of an emerging definition of a profession involving a moral obligation, as well as the obligation to render technically competent service, to those seek-

ing counsel. In the same vein are Vitruvius' views of the duties of the architect, published about 27 B.C. Vitruvius,
architect and military engineer under Caesar and Augustus,
specified honesty, incorruptibility, courtesy, and justice as
indispensable to the reputable and dedicated architect. He must
not be grasping or preoccupied with receiving perquisites and,
if he is to do his job competently, he ". . must receive training in all the departments of learning." Those who aspired to
be architects should be: ". . . skillful with the pencil, instructed in geometry, know much history, have followed the
philosophers with attention, have some knowledge of medicine, know the opinions of the jurists, and be acquainted with
astronomy and the theory of the heavens. . . . I think that
men have no right to profess themselves architects hastily,
without having [been] . . . nursed by the knowledge of many
arts and sciences. . . . *For a liberal education forms, as it were,
a single body made up of these members.*"[22]

Vitruvius, in this remarkable passage, seems to regard liberal education and preprofessional education as one and the
same, much as Galen did at a later date. But Galen provided
no curricular detail[23] and, influential though his views came
to be in later centuries, he had little influence on Roman
medical education, which was, for the most part, haphazard
and disorganized.[24]

Scribonius Largus and Professio. Rome's all-important contribution to medicine was to begin its transformation from a
Greek craft to a profession in something like the present-day
sense: Roman authors began to dilute guild rules of conduct
for members of the healing vocation with principles that fo-
cused on the needs and rights of patients. The enormous significance of this development seems to have been underesti-
mated by most accounts of the history of the concept of

profession and professional ethics, the main exception being Ludwig Edelstein.[25]

There are suggestions of the development in Cicero's *De Officiis* (written 46–43 B.C.), in which the author refers to physicians directly or by inference a number of times. In referring to medicine (as a calling), Cicero regularly uses the word *ars*, not *professio*.[26] In the famous dialogue between Diogenes and Antipater, Cicero firmly backs Antipater and, in words that bring Amos's justice-righteousness (law-ethics) spectrum to mind, condemns the practice of abstaining from ". . . doing for one's own profit only what the law expressly forbids." He speaks of practices that are not forbidden by statute or civil law, but that are nevertheless forbidden by moral law.[27] He also cites Plato's view that the first ethical concern of the ruler is to place the good of the people above his own interests; the ruler is the servant of the people, not the other way round.[28] But Cicero's main thought seems to have been Stoic rather than Platonic.[29]

It was, however, a Roman physician of the first century A.D. who clearly recognized the physician's obligation to place his patient's interests above loyalty to the medical guild. The physician was Scribonius Largus, possibly the son of a slave, who may have accompanied the Emperor Claudius to Britain in A.D. 43. In the introduction to a work designed to emphasize the therapeutic importance of drugs, Scribonius very clearly characterized medicine as a calling with an ethical commitment focusing on the patient,[30] and seems to have been the first to designate medicine as a profession *(professio)* in this sense. In his eyes, medicine was more than a mere craft *(techné* to the Greek, *ars* to the Roman).

Scribonius speaks of Hippocrates as the founder of the profession which, he adds, was the first to be bound by a sacred oath.[31] The true physician must treat all and sundry—

rich and poor, friend and enemy—alike; he must do no harm; he must be learned in his profession. The physician who withholds efficacious drugs for any reason, whether because of the sin of envy or fear of exposure of ignorance, and who lacks a full measure of compassion and love of mankind[32] ought to be abhorred by gods and men. "Where there is no love of people, and where good and bad are given the same value . . ." medicine is degraded and, in a sense ceases to be a profession.[33] *Humanitas* and a high level of specific technical knowledge are standards imposed by the profession itself, and are part of its ethical commitment. It is not so much the desire for money or glory as the desire for knowledge of the science and, by inference, *humanitas*, that motivates the true physician.[34] Medicine is the knowledge of healing, not of hurting, and fails to live up to its promises if it ". . . does not try in every way to help the sick."[35]

Casual mention is made of the *Oath* attributed to Hippocrates (specifically, the allusion is to the rule against the use of abortifacients), but at no point is the *Oath* referred to as a comprehensive ethical guide for the physician. Scribonius supplies, in part by the use of the word *professio*, what the *Oath* conspicuously lacks: emphasis on "the ethical connotations of work, the idea of an obligation or a duty on the part of those engaged in the arts and crafts,"[36] an obligation that, by inference, is to patients first, to guild and medical colleagues second.

How widely Scribonius' concept of a profession was known in his own time is unclear, but Seneca, a contemporary and himself a Stoic philosopher, seems to have held views that were somewhat similar. In *De Beneficiis* Seneca says that money paid physicians is in recognition ". . . of their devotion in serving us, in putting aside their own interests and giving their time to us." He also speaks of physicians giving more attention than is professionally necessary; to them, he adds, ". . . no service [is] . . . too burdensome, none too distasteful for him to perform."[37] Stoic philosophy is reflected in a poem, written a little later, that deals with one aspect of the physician's duty: he must ". . . be like God, savior especially of slaves, paupers, rich men, princes; and to all a brother . . . For we are all brothers."[38]

Thus, the definition of a profession in terms of its ethical, supralegal, obligation to the patient—that which Edelstein calls medical humanism—turns out, for all practical purposes, to be based largely on Stoic tenets and was not clearly set out until Scribonius Largus did so about the middle of the first century A.D. It may never have gained wide acceptance in the ancient world, and seems to have gone into eclipse about the time the Roman Empire was divided into eastern and western parts (A.D. 395). One reason may be that guild-like medical organizations in Rome were small and probably unable to impose rules of conduct of any sort on members. We know that there were organizations of professors of medicine and associations of physicians organized as small craft guilds.[39] An edict of Vespasian speaks of the "profession sacred to Apollo and Asculapius, holy and godlike, and authorized to form associations for its own security and solidarity."[40]

But Rome's physicians never reached the top of the social ladder, a position preempted by the patrician class. It was this class, according to one authority, that "gave the Empire its brilliant aspect." Members of the liberal professions, including doctors and teachers, were petit bourgeois, a step below—and a large step at that—the top of Rome's social heap. The lowest was the city proletariat: the free wage earners and a few special types of slaves.[41]

By the third or fourth century A.D., Roman creativity had for the most part run its course. In law and medicine, codifiers and commentators were the rule. It was to certain of them that Justinian's scholars turned in A.D. 528 for the compilation of the great *Corpus Juris*.[42]

There is no work of comparable sweep and influence in medicine, which, in a technical sense, rested on the authority of Galen for a thousand years after the collapse of the western empire. And although Galen was very insistent that the physician should know his technical business well, and although he quoted several of Scribonius' prescriptions, he appears to have made no mention of the ideas set out by Scribonius in his preface. Nor did Galen concern himself with the *Oath* attributed to Hippocrates; he failed, in fact, to mention it at all.

After Rome: Law in Europe in the Dark and Middle Ages. Edward Gibbon, whose magnum opus appeared two centuries ago but still commands respect and a measure of authority, said that the ruin of Rome was due to the injuries of time and nature, the attacks of barbarians and Christians, the use and abuse of materials (by which he meant the greed for gold and silver, among other things), and the Romans' own domestic quarrels.[43] Tending to blame Christian zealotry more than barbarian destructiveness, Gibbon's views have been dismissed by some twentieth-century historians as simplistic and obsolete. However, his interpretation of the exceedingly complex sequence of events that transpired between the accession of Commodus in A.D. 180 and the deposition of Romulus Augustulus in A.D. 476 is not substantively different from the views of later authors having access to important archaeologic and other discoveries of the nineteenth and twentieth centuries. Rome had sustained raids and sackings several times in its long history and had recovered, often with remarkable speed, from most of them. But it suffered symbolic and lasting damage in the sixth century during struggles with the Ostrogoths, Lombards, and Byzantines.

J. B. Bury's classic account of Rome's eclipse describes vast swirlings of various Teutonic and Asiatic peoples round and about the borders of the Roman Empire, beginning with the defeat by the Goths of the Emperor Decius near the mouth of the Danube in A.D. 247 and ending with the invasion of Italy by the Lombards, beginning in A.D. 568.[44] Richard Mansfield Haywood identifies the beginning of the loss of the West with the invasion of Gaul and Spain by the Vandals and others in A.D. 406 and after; the final stage in the process was the conquest by Clovis of the residue of Roman territory in Gaul in A.D. 507.[45] Haywood declines, however, to attribute the process, as did the early (and hostile) Christians, to moral degradation of the sort so avidly described by Suetonius. "There was," says Haywood, "no falling-off in the quality of men . . . no phenomena . . . characteristic of [biologic] old age . . . no failure of nerve. The whole process may be described by ordinary historical methods."[46]

Even with the passage of the western empire under the control of the Ostrogoths and other Teutons, Roman institutions did not die.[47] Some of the new rulers attempted, in fact, to preserve compilations of Roman law for surviving Romans while, at the same time, installing Teutonic customs and law for themselves. For Romans living in Gaul under Clovis, for example, Roman local government was left intact, and the law and law courts of Rome were still the basis of justice.[48]

Of the laws promulgated by barbarian conquerors after the fall of Rome's last western emperor, the laws of the Visigoths are of special interest, since some of them contain provisions relating to the practice of medicine. The Visigothic kingdom began with Euric's seizure of power in A.D. 466, and was obliterated in A.D. 711 by the forces of Islam. Euric promulgated a code of law in A.D. 476; many later Visigothic rulers did likewise. Prominent among these various codes was Alaric's Breviary (Lex Romanum Visigothorum). Promulgated in A.D. 506, it was mainly Roman in content, and was possibly known in Britain in the sixth century.[49] The most comprehensive body of Visigothic law, which drew extensively on previous codes, including Euric's and Alaric's, was the Lex Visigothorum, usually attributed to Ervig (A.D. 681).[50]

Sometime between the promulgation of the Lex Romanum Visigothorum (A.D. 506) and the Lex Visigothorum (A.D. 681), several provisions relating to physicians were introduced.[51] The laws required that a near relative be present if a physician subjected a female patient to venesection. There was also a provision that treatment might be under contract and if, under such circumstances, the patient died, the physician received no fee. Without a contract, the physician bore no liability in the event of adverse effect. If, however, the physician bled a slave, and thus caused weakness or death, he was required to replace the slave. But, unlike most other freedmen, the physician could not be imprisoned without a hearing.[52] Other additions to Visigothic law, presumably promulgated after the Visigoths were converted to Arian Christianity, were designed to discourage or prevent practices leading to abortion. Roman law was only casually interested in the topic, since it did not consider destruction of an unborn child by doctor, midwife, or pregnant woman necessarily illegal.[53]

One of the concerns common to most Visigothic codes was the replacement of the law of talion (an eye for an eye, tooth for tooth, etc.) and the principle of self-help with orderly systems of compensation under the authority of the state. Tables of compensation—specified sums of money for specific injuries, the amount depending on the severity of the injury—and the principle of the *wergeld* are present or implicit in all of them. The *wergeld*, which was the amount to be paid surviving family members in case of homicide, varied according to social status. For example, the Burgundian Code (A.D. 476–516) fixed the amount to be paid to the owner by anyone causing the death of an ordinary slave at thirty solidi. The death of a nobleman, however, required payment of ten times that amount.[54]

Roman law, even in its vulgarized form, began finally to be displaced by Teutonic law with the establishment of the Lombard kingdoms in Italy, which promulgated their own law codes.[55] In later centuries, Frankish kings allowed Lombard law to remain in effect when they gained control of the Lombard kingdom, and Lombard law, although much altered, was not entirely displaced until the twelfth century when Roman law based on the rediscovered Digest of Justinian began to take over.

Early Teutonic Law. In those areas of northern Europe that were never (or only briefly) occupied by the Romans, bodies of customary law developed which were uninfluenced by Roman law. The areas in question lay mostly in what is now northern Germany and Denmark, and were inhabited largely by Teutonic tribes. Tacitus, writing in the first century A.D., tells us that Teutonic tribes in Germany traditionally espoused an ascending theory of government, decisions on major matters being reached by an assembly of all the people. Teutonic law required death sentences only for traitors, cowards, and what may have been homosexuals. Traitors were hanged but the two other categories, whose offenses were considered more shameful, were executed by burial alive in bogs. Ironically, their physical remains have survived those of the traitors; the bodies of "bog people," executed by strangulation, have been recovered intact in our own time. All other offenses required the payment of compensation by the wrongdoer both to the injured party and to the king. Payment was in horses or cattle, there being no coinage. "Even homicide," says Tacitus, "can be atoned for by a fixed number of cattle or sheep, the compensation being received by the whole family."[56] Tacitus makes no mention of law or custom relating specifically to healers or healing; he does point out, however, that treatment of battle wounds was mainly in the hands of women.[57]

Tacitus' *Germania* was completed in A.D. 98, and drew on several previous authors whose works, with one exception, are now lost. The exception is Ceasar's *The Gallic War*, in which the Teutonic tribes are described as hunters and gatherers, opposed to agriculture, and existing mainly for warfare.[58] As will be seen, it was the primitive law of the Teutons that reached Britain as the Romans were departing (fifth century A.D.), and that was the base on which later bodies of law were built. Not for many centuries would Roman law begin to influence English common law.

4 · The Common Law of Malpractice and London's Medical Guilds

Roman control of Britain lasted from 55 B.C. to A.D. 410 and, at one time or another, extended to the entire island except the far north and the far west. The Romans had the good sense to leave Ireland to its own devices, although Agricola at one time considered an Irish adventure.[1]

Rome's legacy to Britain was more physical than otherwise. Roads, buildings, and cities remained after the legions departed, but the nonphysical evidence of Rome's presence, including such of its law as may have been applied in Britain, disappeared with astonishing rapidity. Roman law was in effect in Britain, but the extent to which it applied to natives, whose mother tongue was Celtic, is uncertain. There are records of imperial rescripts pertaining to Romans stationed in Britain, but the volume of such records is surprisingly small.[2]

With the departure of the Romans, the establishment of law based on Teutonic custom was not long in coming, owing to the arrival of three shiploads of Teutons (Angles, Saxons, and

Jutes) from north of the mouth of the Elbe in A.D. 446 or a bit later.[3] The law and custom they brought is thought to be the same as, or very similar to, that described by Tacitus in his *Germania* (chapter 3). From such antecedents, early English law took off on its own. The earliest compilation after the Teutonic invasion was a haphazard collection of customary law compiled by King Aethelbert of Kent, England's first Christian king, about A.D. 600, and is remarkable primarily in that it is said to have been the first document of consequence to have been written in English. A century or so later the laws of Ine (ruled from 688 to 726) and Alfred of Wessex (born 849, died 899) were reduced to writing. Still later came the laws of Aethelred and Canute, which were largely revisions, with additions, of the earlier collections. Canute's was the last collection of Anglo-Saxon law prior to the Norman Conquest.[4]

Teutonic law as adopted by pre-Conquest Britain made little attempt to distinguish between what are now called civil and criminal offenses, and went to great lengths to bring the various forms of self-help under judicial supervision. As in earlier Teutonic law, the offender in most cases (including homicide) could buy his way out by compensating the injured party or his survivors.

Damage to some types of property, as well as theft, were compensable by specified sums. So was injury to the person. Alfred's laws listed fifty-five types of personal injury along with the exact sums to be paid for each by the offender to the injured party. The sums depended in some cases on the worth of the life of the person suffering the injury (the wergeld); in other cases they seem to have been more arbitrary. Loss of the first finger, for example, brought fifteen shillings and the little finger only nine. The big toe was worth twenty shillings and the little toe only five. An eye was worth sixty-six shillings and a nose sixty.[5] In one of Aethelbert's laws,[6] compensation was allowed for medical treatment made necessary by personal injury, but apart from this doctors and healers are not mentioned, as such, anywhere in Anglo-Saxon law.

The final version of Anglo-Saxon law was King Canute's compilation, probably promulgated between 1027 and 1034, which was both comprehensive and unoriginal in that it drew very heavily on earlier versions. Canute's laws were translated, revised, rearranged, and renamed by later authors, some of them writing after the Conquest. William the Conqueror had the good sense to reaffirm and expand them, identifying them, except for his own additions, as the laws his cousin King Edward the Confessor had observed before him.[7]

Anglo-Saxon law is said to have set the stage for the English concept of kingship, for later English administrative divisions and land laws, and possibly for trial by jury. Perhaps most important of all, it accustomed Englishmen of Saxon and Danish origins to compromise in the settlement of private conflicts under the eye of the courts. The alternative was settlement by private vengeance, as in ancient law, if the offender could not or would not pay the injured party's wergeld or appropriate fraction thereof. There were, of course, crimes that could not be propitiated by payment of money, but most instances of personal injury could be dealt with in this way. Compensation of the injured party by the wrongdoer was thus a well-established legal principle in Britain well before the Conquest, but the Roman concept of *delictum* and lawful and unlawful injury *(iniuria)* slumbered on in manuscripts of Justinian's *Digest*, buried and forgotten in continental archives.

Post-Conquest: Henry de Bracton. Some English historians claim that England before the Norman Conquest was a unified, happy, prosperous nation, and that the Normans, being relatively uncultured, brought chaos which persisted until the English natives could educate their conquerors to civilized ways.[8] Continental historians manage to convey the opposite point of view.[9] Whatever the truth of it, the rapid centralization of political and judicial authority in England in the two centuries after the Norman Conquest must be counted one of the administrative miracles of the Christian era. As a result, England became a strongly unified nation long before her continental neighbors and, partly as a consequence, was able to influence the development of the Western world out of all proportion to her geographic size.

It would, in theory, have been easier after the Conquest to take over the Roman law more or less intact. That, indeed, might have happened had not Teutonic law been imposed in the early English kingdoms soon after the Romans departed. But, perhaps most important, the Roman law had not reemerged at the time of the Conquest, and Norman conquerors brought little or no written law with them. Roman law, as we have seen, had survived the fall of Rome piecemeal and in corrupt form here and there on the continent, and its reemergence in the twelfth century in coherent and systematic form (especially Justinian's *Digest*) came too late to dominate the basic processes that were to produce the English common law. In their earliest phases, those processes are far from clear, but near the end of the thirteenth century the common law process was beginning to generate a literature to replace written versions of Anglo-Saxon law.[10] The Anglo-Saxon laws, as we have seen, were collections of individual statutes designed for specific circumstances, especially those having to do with disputes between individuals. The common law process, quite early in its history, began to depend on prior judicial decisions in the King's Courts and thus required a new type of legal record.

Sometime during the reign of Edward I (acceded 1272, died 1307), legal scribes began to record decisions taken in the King's Courts, thus originating the Year Book series, a unique legal and social record that extends to the time of Henry VIII with very little interruption.[11] As will be seen, the Year Book record of the fourteenth century throws considerable light on the status of physicians and surgeons in England at that time. But the break with the Anglo-Saxon legal tradition occurred before the Year Book series began and was clearly signalled by Henry de Bracton's monumental *On the Laws and Customs of England*, written sometime between 1239 and 1258. Not much more than a century earlier, the written law in force was *Leges Henrici Primi*, the wergeld was still in use, and injury was compensated according to a fixed schedule, as it had been in Alfred's day. None of this was present in Bracton's opus. In its place were large portions of the basic common law of England, not yet fully fleshed out but radically different from the Anglo-Saxon system. Bracton's work also brought Roman law to Britain, especially where actions for damages were concerned. Holdsworth acknowledged Bracton's great role by assigning nearly fifty pages to him in his second volume. Commenting on Bracton's use of Roman legal principle, he observed that

It is in [his] section dealing with obligation and actions that the influence of Roman law appears on the surface. . . . There was nothing in English law equivalent to the Roman concept of *obligatio* . . . [although] English law was beginning to get a scheme of actions of its own. . . . He deals with many questions relating to obligation and contract, fraud, and negligence, about which the common law had as yet no rules. In dealing with these matters he necessarily uses Roman terms and borrows Roman rules.[12]

Bracton's section entitled *Obligations arise ex delicto or quasi* sets the stage. "Everything wrongfully done," he says in Justinian terms, "may be called *iniuria*. . . ." If there is willful intent, it is *ex maleficio;* otherwise it is trespass, the equivalent of tort in medieval English terminology. And, with reference to the latter, he adds: "An *iniuria* may amount to a trespass, as where something is done contrary to the statutes of the king and kingdom by excluding mean and measure or by doing less than what is due, that is, less than he ought, through malice and fraud or negligence and neglect." Bracton's phrase *mean and measure* may be taken as an approximation to the present-day due care and skill.[13] If there is intent to injure, the matter becomes criminal. But the inference is that certain individuals (e.g., physicians or veterinarians) may inflict injury while engaged in a lawful professional act and are liable for damages only if they ". . . do not employ due care. . . ."[14] Bracton thus brings English common law abreast, in some respects, of Roman law at its peak of development. Roman jurists of the classical period had reached a point at which certain relations between parties implied certain duties; a professional or a provider ". . . might be held to a standard of action because an upright and diligent man . . . would so act."[15]

As for determination of damages, injury (Bracton says *iniuria* in this particular context) ". . . may be grievous or slight, and accordingly a heavier or lighter punishment will follow . . ." against the wrongdoer. It is the judge who will ". . . condemn the wrongdoer to pay a sum as large as that for which the plaintiff has said he would not have suffered the harm, . . ."[16] a view that is reminiscent of Talmudic principles and, however defective, is at least as rational as the reasoning used by some modern juries in arriving at the amounts to be paid in damages by the wrongdoer to the injured party.

Bracton's major work thus seems to fix the origins of common law concepts approximately in the twelfth and early thirteenth centuries, prior to which the old Anglo-Saxon concepts of wergeld and tables of compensation still prevailed. Bracton's work was thus a bridge between classical Roman law and the emerging English common law.

By the beginning of the fourteenth century, common law was well established. The turbulence of the two centuries immediately following the Conquest had left their mark, but were largely a thing of the past. So also was Henry II's clash with Beckett and the Roman Church.[17] The King's Courts (King's Bench, Common Pleas, Chancery, and Exchequer) were meeting in their assigned corners of William II's awesome Westminster Hall.[18]

The King's Courts were beginning to loom larger in the lives of Englishmen than the many local courts, some of them very ancient. But complaints brought before the King's Courts had to fit, more or less precisely, into one of a series of rigidly defined writs; if there were no writs into which a particular complaint could be fitted, the bearer of the complaint could not gain a hearing. In early common law, one such writ was trespass, which usually meant a wrong for which monetary compensation was sought.[19] A special variety of the trespass writ (trespass on the case) was the means by which most actions for compensation for injury caused unintentionally by physicians were admitted for trial in one of the Kings' Courts, usually Common Pleas.[20]

The earliest actions seeking compensation for injury that were brought against physicians probably took place in local courts and were unrecorded. The earliest surviving record of what may reasonably be called a malpractice action bears the date 1329 and was decided by one of the king's circuit courts, themselves established as a means of extending the king's power beyond Westminster to the most remote parts of the kingdom. The record is scanty and fails to provide the names of the parties (plaintiff and defendant), but the judge was William de Denum (Denom), appointed by Edward III early in his reign. A healer of some sort, in treating an eye ailment with herbs, allegedly caused the loss of the eye. The patient brought suit, using the trespass writ. This, said counsel for defence, was technically improper; Denom agreed. His comment was as follows:

I saw a case where a man in Newcastle was arraigned before me and my associate Justices assigned, for the death of a man, and I asked the reason for the indictment and it was said that he [physician] had injured a man [patient] who was under his care, so that he [patient] died four days later. When I saw that he [physician] was a man of that occupation, and did not do the thing feloniously but against his will, I told him to go on his way. I put it to you that if a smith, who is [also] a man of occupation, drives a nail into your horse's hoof so that you lose your horse, you will never have recovery against him [smith]. Nor shall you here.[21]

Justice Denom's implication was that if the physician or veterinarian, acting within the usual professional relationship, injures or kills the patient (human being or horse) but does not intend to do so, he is not liable. Negligent or ignorant conduct would, therefore, not impose liability. The patient thus put himself in his physician's hands at his own peril. Early English common law seems to have followed somewhat the same principle, vis-à-vis physicians, that is evident in Greek law of the fourth and fifth centuries B.C.

A year after Denom's decision, another of the king's circuit courts, heard a case in which John the Warner had been wounded in an assault and sought treatment at the hands of Thomas the Leech.[22] Thomas agreed to cure him within five weeks, and a payment by John of one and a half silver marks sealed the unwritten agreement. Within two days Thomas abandoned his patient, who then had to seek treatment from

another physician to whom he paid £5 for professional services. A jury supported the patient's view of the matter and
awarded him £10 damages.

Several additional cases of actions for malpractice against
physicians are to be found in records of local courts in mid-
century. Two of them, one from Devonshire and one from
Cheshire, are of interest primarily because they suggest that
local courts, possibly influenced by local feeling, may have
dealt much more severely with medical wrongdoers than the
King's Courts. The punishment in one case was outlawry and
in the other loss of all "goods and tenements," both unusually severe penalties for a noncriminal offense.[23]

To this point, records of actions against physicians disclose
little evidence of the emergence of a unique law of professional malpractice; they do suggest, however, a growing
awareness by the courts and the public of a distinct healing
profession and of the need to compensate patients injured accidentally by careless physicians. But by the middle and latter part of the fourteenth century, the status of both physicians and veterinarians in the eyes of the law had begun to
change. The altered status is clearly seen in what is usually
called The Surgeon's Case of 1375, also known as *Stratton v.
Swanlond*.[24] Robert and Agnes of Stratton, man and wife, sued
John Swanlond, a surgeon, who had treated Agnes's wounded
hand with unsatisfactory therapeutic results. The Plea Rolls
of King's bench say that Swanlond guaranteed "well and
competently" to cure the wound, an allegation that he denied. Instead, he claimed, he reattached a hand that was virtually severed, but did not guarantee a cure.

The report in the Year Book series differs in that it fails to
name the plaintiffs, and assigns what appears to be a mali-
cious pseudonym (J. Mort) to the surgeon. As in the Plea Roll
account, the surgeon is alleged to have been negligent and in

II
Trefpas.
Ley. 36.
Action fi r
le cafe.
Er. 24.
tit. 9.

UJⱰ home poʒt bře de Trefpas fur fon cafe debers un J. Mort' furgeon, ⱪ le bře boile, lou fa maine beſtꝰ fuit bleſſ. per un T. B. q̃ m̃ ceſtꝑ bers qui le bře eſt poʒt, empʒiſt p̃ faner de fon malabie en fa maine, lou per negligence de mefme ceſtꝑ J. ⱪ fa cure, fa maine ē empaire p̃ taunt, q̃ il eſtoit maiheme a toʒt ⱪ a fes damages. Ɐt bſde que en ceſt bʒiefe ne fuit mp̃ fait mention en q̃l lieu il empʒife, ⱪc. ut fupra, mes en fon count il declara, q̃ il fe empʒiſt en Lound' en Towerſtreet, ⱪ en la parothe de B. Ɐt le bře ne fuit mp̃ vi & armis, ne contra pacem, &c. Gafc. Ɉl ne pʒiſt pas de lup faner de fa malady, come il ad fuppofe, pʒiſt a defaire p̃fa lep, ⱪc. ¶ Honning, Ɐeſt un actiō de Ɐrefpas, ⱪ del thofe q̃ thict en confiſance del pais, en q̃l cafe le lep n'eſt mp̃ grauntable, p̃ quop̃ pur default de refpōs no⁹ demādom⁹ judg̃, ⱪ pʒiom⁹ nous damages. ¶ Candiſh Ⱥⱦōⱥs Juſtic̃, ceo bře ne fuppa foʒce ⱪ armes, ne encounter le peace, iſſint q̃ la lep a ceo q̃ femble eſt aſſets acceptable, p̃ quop̃ boilles la lep ou nemp̃, ⱪc. ¶ Hon. Ɱoꝰ ne boilomus accept la lep pur riens q̃ puit a beñ.

Ley. 41.

¶ Candiſh, Donques no⁹ recoʒbomus, q̃ refufes la lep, ut fupra. Ɐt jeo die bien, q̃ bo⁹ eſtes en foʒt cafe, q. d. la lep eſt acceptable. Ɐt fic eſt l'opinion de tout la court. Ɐt pur ceo q̃

[B]

le defendaunt bieſt, que il euſt eſtre adjourne tāq̃ a un auter terme, il weiber le tendꝰ de la lep, q̃ il ne impʒiſt pas de [B] garratꝑ fa main, ut fupra, pʒiſt, ⱪc. Ɐt alii è [B] contra. ¶ Gaf. Ɒʒe fir bo⁹ beics bien, coū̃t le bře ne fait pas mention en quel lieu il en pʒiſt de lup garratꝑ, iſſint eſt ceſt bře defectibe en matter, car le court ne puit mpe fcaber

Briefe. 6.
27. Br. 501

de q̃l bifne de faire beſt le pais. ¶ Perfay, Ɉl n'ab mp̃ lim:t le lieu en le bře, p̃ quop̃ nous demaunde judg̃ de bře. ¶ Hon', Ɒur ceo nous abomus aſſigñ en noſtꝰ coūt le lieu, en q̃l il empʒiſt de no⁹ garrātie, iſſint c̃ q̃ n'eſt mp̃ compʒife deins le bře, eſt compʒife deins le count, ⱪ ceo nous doit fuffic̃ a cel regarꝺ, de faire bener le pais del lieu, ou nous abomus affirme l'enpʒendꝰ, p̃ q̃ judg̃, fi nře bře ne foit aſſets bon. ¶ Candiſh, Ɒʒe eſt il temps de challenge le bře, p̃ c̃ q̃ il n'ab mp̃ lup aſſigñ, ou le thofe duiſt eſtre enpʒife, pur c̃ q̃ il co= bient de faire bener le pais de cel lieu, ⱪc. mes ſi bo⁹ uſſes demurre fur la lep folonq̃ noſtꝰ pʒimer iſſue, Ɐt la lep acceptable, donques ne cobient de aber aſſigne lieu per le bře. Ɐt aurꝑ ceſt action de cobenāt pur neceſſitꝑ eſt mainꝰ fauns eſpecialtꝑ, pur ceo que pur ꝑ petit thofe home ne puit mp̃ aꝺ tout temps Ɐlerke pur faire efpecialtꝑ, per quop̃. ¶ Ham. Le bře fuppofe q̃ il eſt maibem per lup, iſſint q̃ il eſt fuppofer, q̃ per le nature de cel bʒebe il ferra befoigñ, q̃ liew fuiſt. compʒife, p̃ quop̃, ⱪc. ¶ Candiſh, Ɉl n'eſt mp̃ maybeme p̃ lup, eins p̃ un auꝰ q̃ lup fert̃, iſſint q̃ fi il recober damages a oʒe debers le defendꝰ, il abera auꝰ= foits un Appell̃ debers celup, que lup maybeme. ¶ Hon. Ꝓi jeo baile mon thibal a un fer= rour de fert̃, ⱪ'il enclop̃ mon thibal, jeo abeꝰ bře de Ɐrefpas debers lup, ou mon thibal foit bleſſ. per enclober, ⱪ jeo baile mon thibal a Ɱarſhall̃ a garrātꝑ, ⱪ per fa negligent cure mon thibal eſt maibem, j'abeꝰ mefme bʒebe fur le matter, fic in propofito. ¶ Candiſh, Ɐeſt beritꝑ, pur que le thibal ne poit mp̃ aber action, ceſtaſcaboiet Appell̃ de maibeme debers ceſtp̃ q̃ lup feruſt, ⱪc. Ꝓes en ceſt cafe le feme puit aber appele de maibeme debers ceſtp̃ q̃ lup ferruſt. Ɐt fi un ferrour empʒent de garrāt mon thibal. Ɐt fi per negligence de lup ou lachos de fa cure en temps reafonable le thibal eſt impaire, il eſt reafon q̃ il foit culp̃. Ꝓes s'il fait taunt q̃ il puit, ou mitter tout fa diligence de lup cure, il n'eſt pas reafon q̃ il foit ent culp̃, mefq̃s il ne foit garris, car il eſt graunde diberſitie enter les deuꝑ caufes. Ɐt puis p̃ ceo q̃ le lieu fault en le bʒiefe, ou la cure duiſt aber eſtre empʒife, le fuit abaꝺ⁹ per agꝰ. Ɐt le pl' fuit amertc̃ie.

Stratton v. Swanlond. *Y.B. 48 Edw. 111, 1375, f.6, pl. 11.* This version appeared in the *Year Book* series published in London by Sawbridge, et al., in *1679.* The language is Law French. The statement of Cavendish, quoted in translation in the text, begins six lines from the bottom (*Et si un ferrour,* etc.).

breach of unwritten covenant. There is a mass of technical legal detail, which is not at present germane, but highly pertinent was the reasoning of Chief Justice John Cavendish, who used a horse-doctor analogy to make his point: "And if a smith undertakes to cure a horse, and the horse is harmed by his negligence or failure to cure in a reasonable time, it is just that he should be held liable. *But if he does all he can and applies himself with all due diligence to the cure*, it is not right that he should be guilty therefor, [even] though there is no cure. . . ."[25]

Cavendish, reflecting Bractonian influence, said that the professional provider is liable if he is negligent and does not employ "all due diligence" in treating his patient. This is a far cry from Denom's earlier view that the physician is liable, when injury or death results from treatment, only if he intends to do harm. Future precedent was to follow the Cavendish view, which implies a reasonable standard of performance below which the physician must not fail if he is to escape liability for damages when his treatment causes injury. There is as yet no mention of "ordinary knowledge and skill," although they may be implicit in the proviso ". . . if he does all he can. . . ." The highly significant differences between malfeasance, with its suggestion of evil intent and criminal overtones (which was Denom's criterion), and misfeasance, which is "the improper performance of some act which a man may lawfully do," was obviously recognized by both Denom and Cavendish, although the terms themselves were not introduced until the sixteenth century. Yet to come was the concept of liability for nonfeasance: failure to act when professional duty requires it, a concept that was well-recognized in Roman law of the classical period.

Cavendish, who was beheaded during the Peasants' Revolt of 1381 when the mob demanded the death of "all lawyers, all the men of the Chancery and the Exchequer and everyone who could write a writ or a letter",[26] may have been influenced by two earlier cases, in both of which negligence by a veterinarian was alleged or implied.[27] In all these fourteenth-century Year Book cases, the intense preoccupation of English justices with the form and language of writs is painfully apparent. In any event, *Stratton v. Swanland* may, with some justification, be considered the first significant malpractice case in English common law, even though it finally turned on a technicality rather than on substantive law. One can, using standard legal records and references, trace many modern British and American malpractice cases back to it in unbroken line.[28]

After cessation of the Year Book Series, legal reporting was taken up by individual law reporters; the earliest were Dyer (1537–1582), Plowden (1550–1580), and Coke (1572–1616). But very little of direct interest where professional malpractice is concerned seems to have been extracted from them. Francis Bacon, in his *Maxims* of the law (1630), said that if a man is hurt or maimed by the inadvertant action of another, ". . . though it be against the party's mind and will, he shall be punished . . . as deeply as if he had done it of malice. . . . So if a surgeon authorized to practice do through negligence in his cure cause the party to die, the surgeon shall not be brought in question for his life; and yet if he do only hurt the wound, whereby the cure is cast back, and death ensues not, he is subject to an action upon the case for his misfeasance."[29] A century late, the ambiguities in Bacon's maxim were no longer manifest. The principles of medical malpractice had begun to assume their present form and compass:[30] the man of medicine does not guarantee a cure and must observe customary, or average, standards of practice. He is not required to measure up to the most refined standards. He need not be a genius or stand at the head of his profession; his practice must be comfortably and demonstrably average.

Physicians and Their Guilds. The state of the healing vocation in Britain during, and for some centuries after, the Roman occupation is not well documented. The Venerable Bede mentioned Cynifrid, a physician who tended Queen Edilthryd in her terminal illness about A.D. 179. More significantly, he spoke many times of Anglo-Saxon leeches.[31] But according to Edward J. Kealey, only eight physicians (*medici*) can be identified by name in English records from the departure of the Romans to the Norman Conquest (1066). From the Conquest to the middle of the twelfth century (1154), 103 physicians can be identified, nearly half having been monks or clerics of some sort. Most bore Norman names.[32] In the twelfth century there is record of an apothecary, probably not a priest, who accompanied Henry II on a journey to Ireland and about a century later one "john le spicer, aut apotecarius" was Mayor of York.[33] For a time, the apothecaries were associated with the Spicers and Pepperers which, after much strife, became the Company of Grocers by royal charter in 1428.[34] This, in turn, gave way to the Master, Wardens and Society of the Art and Mystery of the Apothecaries of the City of London in 1617, by charter granted by King James in 1616.[35]

The intricate process by which London's physicians managed to elevate their tribe above all other healers is not easily explicable, but it had something to do with claims of higher education and competence. Physicians were gentlemen and educated; surgeons and apothecaries were unlettered craftsmen, not admissible to the ranks of the gentry. For all that, it probably made little difference to the patient except for the fee he was required to pay. The medieval physician's knowledge of Galen was, in effect, hardly more valid than the apothecary's knowledge of herbs.

In any case, thirteenth-century London society was, in general, rigidly stratified;[36] the stratification was firmly built into London's system of craft guilds on which model the physicians, for very good reason, constructed their own guild early in the sixteenth century.

London's Royal College of Physicians. When Henry VIII ascended the throne (1509), there was a well-developed stratum of lesser gentry, which included some lawyers, physicians (but not surgeons or apothecaries), and some members of the clergy. London's physicians, when the opportunity arose, sought to affirm their position at the top of the healing calling by petitioning the king for a charter and special privileges. The opportunity arose when one of their number, Thomas Linacre, attained special status as physician in the king's court.

Linacre, almost certainly not born to privilege, began his rise to fame and power when he became Fellow at All Soul's, Oxford, about 1484. A few years later he went to Padua, where he received a medical degree in 1496. This, however, may have been the least of his scholarly achievements while in Italy (about 1487 to 1499). The renaissance of classical languages and literature was in full swing, and Linacre profited mightily from the fact. He became, in fact, England's own Renaissance man and, among several others, was responsible for bringing the renewed interest in Greek and Latin of the Renaissance to England. Erasmus had high regard for him as a humanist and scholar, as did other colleagues on the continent.[37] He is also said to have taught Greek to a number of English notables, including Thomas More.[38] He was brought into the court of Henry VIII in 1509 and remained a prominent figure at court for the rest of his life.

How Linacre, along with five other physicians and Thomas Cardinal Wolsey, then Lord Chancellor, came to present a petition to Henry VIII in 1518 to found London's Royal College of Physicians is not clear, but there was a precedent of sorts. Seven years earlier Parliament had passed an Act requiring that anyone desiring to practice medicine in London ("nor within seven miles of it") had to be examined by the Bishop of London or the Dean of St. Paul's, plus four doctors of physic or surgeons.[39] The Act of 1511 was to endure on the books for a very long time; it was not repealed until 1948 and as late as 1827 the Archbishop of Canterbury, apparently without benefit of faculty or college, was still able to award the M.D. degree.[40]

There were other precedents as well. In Rome, a college (actually a corporation) of physicians had begun to regulate the practice of medicine in the early middle ages. Florence had a powerful, guild-like organization of physicians and apothecaries by the thirteenth century. Similar organizations grew up in other Italian cities, and it can hardly be doubted that Linacre came to be familiar with them during the ten or twelve years he spent in Italy.[41]

The petition laid before Henry VIII in 1518 contained justification for the proposed professional organization in the same terms that appeared in the Act of 1511: there was "a great multitude of ignorant persons . . . taking upon them great cures . . . to the grievous hurt, damage, and destruction of many of the King's liege people. . . ." That there were other reasons, mostly having to do with the prosperity and well-being of the physicians themselves, there can be no doubt. But, in the words of the College's official twentieth-century historian, "only a cynic could deny that in the foundation of the College, there was an element of disinterested public spirit."[42] That element, however, was not always apparent in the several centuries following the founding of the College.

The king granted his letter patent on 23 September 1518 and the "College or Commonalty of the Faculty of Medicine of London" (it was later that the title Royal College of Physicians was employed) came into being. The Charter of 1518[43] was confirmed by Act of Parliament in 1523.[44] The Act extended the Charter, specifying that no one could practice physic anywhere in England without the College's license, graduates of Oxford and Cambridge excepted. By 1553, the College had been given authority to send any offender to any prison in the City except the Tower, and to order gaol-keepers to hold him until the College ordered his release.[45]

These were sweeping powers to be granted to a body that was responsible to no public authority, but there were local precedents, equally sweeping, which gave extraordinary powers to guilds, fraternities, and City companies. The College's own rules defined minutely the office of the president, among whose duties was the reading of "the penal statutes" in the presence of the fellows at all regular comitia. There were four censors who must examine, correct, and if necessary prosecute all who proposed to practice medicine in London, and who must also punish wayward apothecaries. In addition, the president had a caduceator, or servant, who might be ordered to apprehend all whom the censors wished to examine.

Thus, the College at its inception was designed to protect the public from quacks and pretenders of all sorts. Its founders, notably Linacre himself, no doubt had a strong sense of obligation to the English public, as well as pride and faith in the new physicians' organization. Later officials of the College saw its obligations quite differently, and set it on a narrow, self-serving course.

Of these officials, the most notable and influential was John Caius. Born in 1510, he was strikingly different in temperament and outlook from Thomas Linacre. Where Linacre was of inquiring, gracious, and studious mind and habit, Caius was crotchety and rigidly authoritarian. Although scholarly enough, Caius's ". . . temper of mind was literary rather than scientific. . . . He always looked backward to the past."[46] To William Osler, Caius was receptive to the new learning of his time but, notwithstanding, had a medieval mind.[47] Osler considered his greatest contribution to be the refounding and refurbishing of Gonville and Caius College at Cambridge. Another author observed that his contributions to medical progress were minimal.[48]

Caius, like Linacre, went to Padua in 1539 for medical training. It was there that he encountered Vesalius, whose anatomical studies showed Galen to have been wrong in many of his assertions. To Caius, Galen was the master, his authority not to be questioned or doubted; not surprisingly, he and Vesalius seem to have disagreed very considerably. Caius saw no harm in new approaches as long as they were not critical of Galen, whose writings, to Caius, needed only proper reconstruction to make medical research quite unnecessary. "I praise diligence," wrote Caius, "if it be well-directed and not critical of a man so great that the world of medicine has had none such since his death nor will have again."[49] Caius became Fellow of the College of Physicians in 1547 and attained the presidency in 1555, an office which he held until 1560. He was then reelected time after time until, after his ninth reelection in 1571, he finally stepped down.

Caius's stamp on the College of Physicians was firm and irreversible. Inordinately fond of ritual, he designed the president's robes and various odds and ends (book of statutes ornamented with silver, a special caduceus, and a silver verge round which snakes wind their way) that figure in the regular ceremonies of the College. It was Caius who required a beadle bearing a mace to precede the president in procession and to address him as "Your Excellency."[50] Under Caius, discipline within the College was strict and punishment could be meted out for all sorts of offenses, including disagreeing with Galen.[51] He was no less zealous in pursuing and punishing practitioners whom the College considered irregular.[52]

Caius may thus be said to have subverted the College in many ways from the noble course Linacre had set for it in 1518. But beyond doubt Caius's most enduring and dubious accomplishment was the confusion he inflicted in the realm of professional ethics. Finding the statutes of the College in disarray, Caius undertook to put them in orderly arrangement. There is a long list of constitutional provisions which are followed by statutes that, according to Clark, were designated penal in 1543. "But out of respect for doctoral dignity, they were designated *ethical* in 1563," almost certainly by Caius.[53] Actually, the document in its version of 1555 begins with the title *Statuta Collegii Mediocorum Londini* and runs for many pages until a section entitled *De Statutis Moralibus Seu Penalibus* (Concerning Ethical or Penal Statutes) is reached.[54] From 1647 to 1835 the corresponding heading became *De Conservatione Morali et Statutis Poenalibus.*[55] The same title appears in the version of the statutes published in 1698. There are twenty-two chapters, the last chapter containing the "penal or ethical" statutes.[56] A version of 1722 contains the same title and content.[57] But a version dated 1882, containing twenty-seven chapters, makes no mention of penal or ethical rules. Instead, chapter XXVI bears the title *Of the Duties and Conduct of Fellows, Members, and Licentiates* under which are listed ten By-Laws.[58]

Examination of the content of these critical chapters in the College's statutes shows that virtually all of the statutes labeled penal or ethical are concerned with fines for infraction of College rules, or with etiquette among physicians. Notable by its absence is direct reference to the interests and welfare of patients. There is no evidence in the statutes of the

College that reflects the advanced thinking of Scribonius' day. To the contrary, members and fellows are instructed to ". . . determine all things to the credit, honour, and perpetuity of the Society," and to ". . . do all things in the practice of your profession for the honour of the college and the good of the public," presumably in that order.[59]

One can only by a major tour de force derive ethical meaning from such admonitions, unless the assumption is that what is good for the profession is, post hoc, also good for the patient. George Clark tacitly recognized the difficulty by stating, without presenting evidence, that the physician ". . . had precepts and principles generally accepted and considered to be morally binding," most of which, he adds, came somehow from the medical classics, including the *Oath* attributed to Hippocrates.[60] To medical men of the time, the *Oath* attributed to Hippocrates seemed to have been symbolic of something good, despite the fact that virtually all its contents was anachronistic or unintelligible or both. Four versions of the *Oath* were printed in England between 1566 and 1597.[61] They differ in content and the several authors who included them in their books did not hesitate to insert concepts that were not in the original version as it has come down to us. With or without such inserts, however, it is difficult to discern from the statutes of the College, penal or ethical, or from its official actions, that members "subordinate . . . their knowledge to an ethical control."[62] Members may have regarded the *Oath* as a convenient symbol with which to impress the layman and the legislator. But their day-to-day professional conduct was most likely guided by the College's penal and ethical statutes, pragmatic devices primarily designed to enhance the status and prosperity of the College itself.

So also was the rigid restriction of the number of Fellows

¶Hippocratis iufiurandum.

Eftor Apollinem medicum, & Aefculapium, Hygiam'q:,& Pa꞉ 'natiam Aefculapij filias, & deos ac deas omnes , me ,quantum in 'me erit,& quantum ingenium meum valebit , hæc omnia obfer= uaturum quæ hoc iureiurando atque his tabellis continentur. Tributurum me præceptori meo à quo hanc artem edoctus fum, non minus quàm parē= tià quo fum genitus,vitam'q; cū eo communicaturum. Res omnes quas illi necelfarias effe intelligam proviribus meis fumminiftraturum : progeniem eius,fratrum loco habiturum:hanc artem fine mercede,& fine pactionibus edocturum. Præcepta omnia liberè & fideliter traditurum, meis & præce= ptoris mei liberis cęterisque difcipulis,qui fe legibus medicinæ adftrinxerit atque iurati fuerint,alij præterea nemini. In curandis ægrotis pro viribus, & pro ingenio meo rebus necelfarijs vfurum , nemini ægritudinem dilatu= rum,nihil per iniuriam facturū. Rogatum mortale venenum nemini datu= rū,neque id cuiꝗ confulturum,neq; mulieri prægnanti ad interficiendū cō ceptum fœtum potionem porrecturum:vitam meam atq; artem meam pu ·ram atq; integram feruaturum:laborātes lapillo haudquaꝗ excifurum , fed expertis huius artis hoc negocium permiflurum : quācunque domum in= greffus fuero,duntaxat liberandis ægrotis operam daturum, omnem iniu꞊ riā,omnem corruptelam,omne genus turpitudinis, res etiā venereas fponte mea euitaturum,fiue muliebria corpora curauero,fiue ví= rilia, fiue hominis liberi,fiue ferui:quæ inter curandum vel videro, vel audiero,vel etiam extra curam in vita ho꞊ minum cognouero,quæ reticenda effe intelli꞊ gam,nemini aperturum, fed intemera/ tam taciturnitatem feruaturum. Præfens igitur iufiuran/ dum integrè atq; incorruptè feruan ti mi hi omnia tam in vita ꝗ in arte mea pro/ fpera fœlicia'q; fuccedāt, & glória in æternum parata fit: tranfgredienti verò atque periuro, contraria omnia eueniant.

A sixteenth-century version of the Oath *attributed to Hippocrates in its "pagan" form. In: Celsus* De re medicum . . . *(Paris, Christian Vuechel, 1529).* COURTESY OF THE NEW YORK ACADEMY OF MEDICINE LIBRARY.

admitted. Prior to 1688 the number was about fifty-five or less; in that year the maximum was raised to eighty, and for the next decade, some effort was made to reach that number. But thereafter the number declined (it was only forty in 1715–16) and remained very low until after the turn of the nineteenth century.[63] It then began to rise and by mid-century was over 160; in 1900 it was 304 and in 1948 it was 747.[64]

Another aspect of the College's record was its relentless use of its authority in its own courts to harass practitioners it considered to be undesirable. Under this authority it punished innumerable offenders, fining some and sending many to prison until, in the early seventeenth century, it came into conflict with a physician who was disposed to fight back. Dr. Thomas Bonham had a medical degree from the University of Cambridge and on this ground he (legally, it would seem) denied that he required the College's license to practice. The College responded by committing him to Fleet Street prison, where he would have remained indefinitely had he not contrived to bring action for false imprisonment. The case that resulted, variously known as Dr. Bonham's Case, College of Physicians' Case, and *Bonham v. Atkins*, became one of the most celebrated in English common law and has been the subject of comment by many legal historians.[65] In the view of the redoubtable Edward Coke, Chief Justice of Common Pleas, the College of Physicians was in conflict of interests, since it pocketed half the fines it collected. Coke went much further, and got himself into political hot water, by adding that when an act of Parliament is "against common right or reason, or repugnant or impossible to be performed," the common law (i.e., the courts) may void such act. In the furor that followed, the principle that emerged triumphant was that acts and statutes of Parliament could be set aside only by Parliament itself.[66] American revolutionaries saw things somewhat differently.[67] Dr. Bonham got out of prison even though Coke's decision was reversed on writ of error by King's Bench. The College moved successfully to reaffirm its extraordinary powers, "lest medicine perish and the empirics triumph."[68] But Bonham's example seems to have encouraged later offenders to defy the College's summons, and as the seventeenth century ran its course, the College had increasing difficulty in enforcing the authority granted it by Henry VIII and Parliament.

Elizabethan Times and After. After the Bonham case, the College meandered on, occasionally attacking empirics of various sorts and resisting as best it could the encroachments of surgeons on medical turf. There was a somewhat enlightened revision of the Statuta Vetera in 1601, prior to which it was still hazardous not to exhibit total fidelity to the authority of Galen. Shortly after the turn of the seventeenth century, the College granted a license to a young physician who was to become its most productive and renowned member. William Harvey, a medical doctor of Padua and Cambridge, was licensed about 1603 and became a fellow in 1607. He was censor in 1613, 1625, and 1629 and treasurer in 1628 (when *De Motu Cordis* appeared) and in 1629. Throughout his life (he died in 1657) he was active in College affairs and he remembered it handsomely in his will.[69] Even so, Harvey seems by his genius and reputation to have done more for the College than the College did for him. His membership triggered no intellectual revolution within the organization, the focus of which was still mostly on social prerogative and professional monopoly. Its battles with competing groups, especially the apothecaries, continued apace with indifferent results. In the late seventeenth century the College hesitated to admit Thomas Sydenham, England's wisest and best-known physician after

Harvey, largely because he had earlier fought in Cromwell's army. He was also suspiciously avant garde in other ways; he, and his close associate John Locke, were reemphasizing observation of the patient in the best Hippocratic tradition and, by so doing, were narrowing the gap between scientific method and medicine.[70] The College, however, was preoccupied with rebuilding after the Great Fire, pursuing its squabbles with empirics and others, and polishing its relations with royalty. Continued unwise and uninspired leadership plagued it through the last years of the century and it entered the eighteenth century heavily in debt, seriously divided within itself, its membership falling, and its influence clearly on the wane.[71] But as late as 1712 it could still send a practitioner to Newgate Prison for twelve weeks and fine him £10 for malpractice.[72]

By the middle of the eighteenth century there were signs that the College was catching up with the times, but the number of fellows was no greater than it had been fifty years earlier. The College still claimed to be supreme among men of medicine on the ground that its members were better educated but the evidence in support of the claim is unimpressive. The College's emphasis was still on Greek, Latin, and Euclid, rather than on learning in the medical field. Its examination was oral and was still conducted in Latin; a candidate might easily come to grief solely because he was unable to conjugate an irregular verb correctly. To the College, education in the proper subjects and at the proper universities must, above all else, produce a gentleman who was acquainted with the social conventions and preferences of England's ruling class. This had a certain justification, since fellows of the College routinely confined their practice to those able to pay their fees; London's poor were still looked after by apothecaries and the emerging new class of general practitioners.[73] Oxford and Cambridge were still the required universities, despite the fact that until the last half of the nineteenth century they were singularly unreceptive to anything resembling what are today known as the biomedical sciences.[74] An early nineteenth-century comment, noting that Henry VIII had granted a monopoly of the practice of physic in London to the College, deplored the abuse of the privilege by the College and said that only the rising expense of bringing actions against apothecaries and empirics in the early nineteenth century had forced the College to mend its ways.[75]

When a modern system of orderly medical education to prescribed levels of qualification came, it was the despised apothecaries, not the exalted physicians, who were chiefly responsible.[76] But before the nineteenth century was out, London's Royal College of Physicians was emerging as a highly respected examining body and its views on the further development of medical education were becoming less conservative and more influential. In 1835 it abolished the centuries-old provision that only graduates of Oxford and Cambridge were eligible to become fellows.[77] Earlier, in 1765, it had decided that its statutes no longer needed to be kept rigidly secret and issued printed copies of them, still in Latin, to all fellows, professors of medicine at Oxford and Cambridge, and licentiates. Just under a century later, they were finally issued in English.[78]

The crescendo of pressure for medical reform that began in the eighteen-thirties finally culminated in definitive legislative action; with it came a dramatic change in the status and powers of London's Royal College. The Medical Act of 1858[79] took from the profession much of its traditional right to prescribe its own educational requirements and made licensure a responsibility of the state which, from that time, controlled listings in the official Medical Register. The College's right to license practitioners in the London area was swept away, as was its authority to fine and imprison offenders in its own courts, an authority that had for the most part long lain dormant.

The most significant feature of the Medical Act of 1858, however, was the establishment of the General Medical Council, a supervisory body to which was assigned control of educational standards and licensure and on which representatives from the Royal College sat, alongside representatives of such plebian bodies as the Apothecaries Society of London, provincial universities (as well as Oxford and Cambridge), and six people nominated by the Crown. There were to be twenty-three members in all, among whom the College nominally possessed no special status or influence.

The passage of the Medical Act of 1858 was a clear break with Britain's past in many important respects. For one thing, it represented the acquisition by government of the control over licensure, which was one important means by which the Physicians' Guild protected its monopoly. In addition, the act removed once and for all the de jure right of a segment of organized medicine to prosecute medical men for various offenses, including failure to obtain the College's license to practice. The conflicts of interest, commented on so vigorously by Edward Coke in Dr. Bonham's case, were finally recognized by the legislature. Parliament, not the profession, now prescribed minimal requirements by statute for education and licensure: The courts were developing minimal standards of professional performance as part of the growing body of the law of torts.

It required many centuries for Britain's politicians and legislators to comprehend that the medical profession, if rendered autonomous by law, would turn its attention primarily to the maintenance of monopoly, financial privilege, and special social status. First the jurists, then the legislators, perceived that the profession's own regulations were not directly concerned with protecting the patient from injury or compensating him after the fact of injury. The courts, and later the legislature, felt it necessary to move into the breach.

Most of these legal precedents were transmitted in some form to the American colonies and to the new nation. So also was the practice of London's Royal College of Physicians of obscuring the fundamental difference between matters ethical and matters procedural, or having to do solely with professional etiquette, doctor-to-doctor. The general principle of considering the fiscal and social welfare of the profession itself to be the physician's *summum bonum* is an attitude that has had a continuous history at least since the Golden Age of Greece. The *Oath* attributed to Hippocrates is a remnant, modified to an unknown degree and for a wide variety of purposes, of that legacy.

5 · From Thomas Percival
to Informed Consent

Britain's Medical Act of 1858 was merely one of many liberal legislative actions that grew out of efforts usually attributed to Jeremy Bentham, Henry Brougham, and others of like political persuasion, all of whom were in turn intellectual products of those eighteenth-century trends collectively known as the Great Enlightenment. Britain's great political Reform Bill of 1832 which, among other things, abolished the infamous "rotten boroughs," was a prominent sign of the times. So also was Bishop Blomfield's proposal in the House of Lords, which set in motion an inquiry into the causes of ill-health among Britain's laboring poor.[1] The ultimate result was the Public Health Act of 1848, which represented the first time Parliament had employed the term *public health* in a legislative action. From that time Britain's central government, acting mostly through local government bodies, took the health of its millions powerfully in hand. The men who actually carried out the will of Parliament, notably Edwin Chadwick, Southwood Smith, and John Simon, inhabited a world that was far removed from the elegant but narrow precincts that were the principal concern of London's Royal College of Physicians.[2] The College continued to serve the medical needs of Britain's nobility and more affluent citizens. England's laboring millions, in sharp contrast, ". . . faced with a social catastrophe they did not understand, impoverished, exploited, herded into slums that combined bleakness and squalor, or into the expanding complexes of small-scale industrial villages, sank into demoralization." Only after 1848, ". . . when the new epidemics began to kill the rich . . ." did action by government became effective and decisive.[3]

But effective and imaginative action was indeed taken, and by the eighties major epidemics of water-borne diseases, notably cholera and typhoid, had ceased altogether, louse-borne typhus occurred only sporadically. It was in all a massive social and legislative achievement by which Britain set the pace for the entire Western world. Considering the nature of the democratic process, the decisions taken were unusually prompt, and the charge that Britain's leaders of the Victorian era, from Canning and Peel to Gladstone and Disraeli, were stubborn and iniquitous defenders of privilege and status quo is plainly absurd and doctrinaire. The charge can, with more justification, be levelled at the stratum of the medical profession represented by London's Royal College of Physicians. Political reform and the entry of government into the field of public health were not matters of primary concern to the College which, if it took any stand at all, inclined toward a negative view. The stirrings of the Enlightenment, the revivals of ancient sophist and stoic concepts defining good citizens as both ruler and ruled, and the political theory of social contract[4] seem not to have entered into the debates of the College's governing bodies. It was accepted as a given that special interests such as the College should enjoy special status, both de facto and de jure. If anything were owed by the College to the public it was to be viewed as a matter of noblesse oblige, a service to be rendered only if the physician-provider saw fit; if rendered, the service warranted extravagant gratitude and financial reward.

The extension of an analogue of the social contract political theory to the professions, notably medicine and law, seems on its face to have been both logical and inevitable in the nineteenth and twentieth centuries, if not earlier. As Harold L. Wilensky, writing in our own time, puts it, there is ". . . a set of moral norms that characterize the established professions. These norms dictate not only that the practitioner do technically competent, high-quality work, but that he adhere to a service ideal; devotion to the client's interests more than personal or commercial profit should guide decisions when the two are in conflict." To which he adds: "The service ideal is the pivot around which the moral claim to professional status revolves."[5] Of particular significance in the present context, Wilensky notes that one of the things a vocation that aspires to professional status must do is to embody ". . . rules to protect clients and emphasize the service ideal . . ." in a formal code of ethics.[6]

This, however, the medical profession as an organized entity, from the time of the Asklepiads to the American Medical Association in the first half of the twentieth century, has had great difficulty accepting. The *Oath* attributed to Hippocrates, the Royal Society's penal and ethical statutes, and the American Medical Association's several codes of ethics are all of a piece: their language, and the politico-economic debate based on them, ". . . have contributed to a public image of guild restrictionism and self-protection,"[7] but not primarily to an image of selfless devotion to a service ideal or to the interests and the needs of the patient.

Thomas Percival and His Successors. In the late eighteenth century, a series of health-related events brought Thomas Percival (1740–1804) of Manchester into meaningful contact with some aspects of physician conduct, and his approach to the matter turned out to be very influential in Britain and America.

Percival came on the scene when in the seventeen-nineties an epidemic of typhoid (or possibly typhus) broke out in Manchester's labor force, mostly employed in the rapidly developing textile industry. The epidemic vastly overtaxed the capacity of the Manchester Infirmary, a charitable institution, and as a consequence the Infirmary's trustees decided to double its professional staff. This was taken as an affront by the existing staff and there followed numerous resignations, charges, and countercharges. The Trustees, casting about for some way to restore order, decided that a thorough revision of an existing body of regulations governing the conduct of the professional staff might be a step in the right direction. To draw up such a document, they turned in 1791 to Percival, who was probably the Institution's most respected staff member.

Percival was born in Lancashire, brought up a Dissenter, and had his early education at Dr. Aikin's Unitarian Academy at Warrington (Lancashire). His medical training was at Edinburgh and at Leiden, an educational sequence that had little in common with the Eton or Harrow, Oxford or Cambridge sequence London's Royal College of Physicians usually required. Indeed, Percival as a Dissenter was ineligible for admission to Oxford or Cambridge and it is probable that, had he applied for admission to London's Royal College as a young man, his qualifications as a gentleman would have been found lacking, however extensive his knowledge of medicine.[8] All this notwithstanding, he was acquainted with many of the great men of his time and, most significantly, corresponded regularly with some of the Enlightenment's most

Thomas Percival (1740–1804) of Manchester. From Edward Brockbank, Sketches of the Lives and Work of the Honorary Medical Staff of the Manchester Infirmary *(Manchester, n.p., 1904).* COURTESY OF THE NEW YORK ACADEMY OF MEDICINE LIBRARY.

prominent figures, including Franklin, Voltaire, and d'Alembert.[9]

Percival, in carrying out the instructions of the Trustees, did precisely as they asked: over the next three years he constructed a well-thought-out set of ground rules for the conduct of professional staff, doctor-to-doctor, within the Infirmary. But, for reasons that are not apparent, he decided not to leave it at that; sometime later, "induced by an earnest desire to promote the honour and advancement of his profession," he decided to extend and enlarge the work, "and to frame a general system of *medical ethics*." The proposed system of rules labelled medical ethics was to ensure ". . . that the official conduct and mutual intercourse of the faculty [staff] might be regulated by precise and acknowledged principles of urbanity and rectitude."[10] The interests of the patient were solely by inference.

Neither the Trustees' request nor Percival's original title[11] had anything to say about medical ethics, but it is abundantly clear that the meaning of the term, when he finally got round to using it, was very much what it had been to John Caius two centuries earlier: the purpose of ethics was to preserve the strength and integrity of the guild and to regulate colleague-to-colleague conduct. The patient's interests could in theory be involved only if one assumed that what was good for the guild was also good for the patient, a proposition that then as now was highly dubious. To the late Chauncey Leake, Percival's *Medical Ethics* was an excellent answer to the needs of the Manchester Infirmary at the time, but was nonetheless "a manual of medical etiquette, an Emily Post guide . . . to proper professional conduct . . . [that was] unfortunately misnamed *medical ethics*."[12]

That Percival drew heavily on the *Statuta Moralia* of London's Royal College there can be no doubt. He tells us as much himself, but he thought the statutes were too limited and invited ". . . the recommendation of a fuller and more adequate code of professional offices."[13] This he unquestionably provided, holding rather strictly to the guild-like purposes of the *Statuta Moralia*. Ironically, had he been writing a few decades earlier, the statutes of London's Royal College would not have been available to him. But by his time, London's Royal College had abandoned its rule of strict secrecy and had given its statutes limited circulation within the profession.[14]

In his preface, Percival cited another source, a nonmedical one, which he praised extravagantly. This was Thomas Gisborne's *On the Duties of Physicians Resulting from the Profession*, a statement that laid down the medical profession's patient-oriented ethical imperative in clear language. Gisborne (1758–1846) was a socially conscious and studious clergyman, educated at Harrow and Cambridge, and personal friend of prominent liberal thinkers of his time. His *On the Duties of Physicians*[15] was a single chapter in a larger work bearing the unwieldly but informative title *An Enquiry into the Duties of Men in the Higher and Middle Classes of Society in Great Britain, Resulting from Their Respective Stations, Professions, and Employments*.[16] In his chapter on physicians, Gisborne discusses rules of professional etiquette, and of gracious doctor-to-doctor conduct, truth-telling in the clinical setting (to which Percival refers), and other matters. Then, setting out his main theme, he says: "Diligent and early attention . . . and an honest exertion of his best abilities are the primary duties which the physician owes to his patient. The performance of them is virtually promised, for he knows that it is universally expected when he undertakes the case of the sick man; and consequently, if he neglects to fulfill them, he is guilty of a direct breach of his engagement."[17] He goes on to say that the physician's concern for the patient's recovery must be un-

A N

E N Q U I R Y

INTO THE

DUTIES OF MEN

IN THE

HIGHER AND MIDDLE CLASSES OF SOCIETY

IN GREAT BRITAIN,

RESULTING FROM THEIR RESPECTIVE STATIONS, PROFESSIONS,
AND EMPLOYMENTS.

BY THOMAS GISBORNE, M. A.

LONDON:

PRINTED BY J. DAVIS,

FOR B. AND J. WHITE, FLEET-STREET.

MDCCXCIV.

influenced by private and personal considerations, and that he must shun "all affectation of mystery."[18]

All of which, taken together, is a considerable departure from the precedent set two thousand years earlier by the *Oath* attributed to Hippocrates, from the spirit and purpose of the *Statuta Moralia* of London's Royal College, and from Percival's own *Medical Ethics*. The notion of unwritten contract between patient and physician, and the primary emphasis on patient's rights, are unmistakable in Gisbourne's treatment but were not carried over into Percival's, despite his extravagant admiration for Gisborne's work.

Percival also cites John Gregory's earlier work on the physician's duties, a statement known to Gisborne. Gregory, less advanced in his thought than Gisborne, described the profession as a liberal one "whose object is the life and health of the human species to be exercised by gentlemen of honour and ingenious manners."[19] He also had a great deal to say about medical etiquette, the use and misuse of the Hippocratic corpus (but no mention of the *Oath*), and the urgent need to write English well. Percival, having praised both works and especially Gisborne's, dismissed them with the comment that their plan and many of their objects differed from his own; but he expressed the hope that the several works would ". . . rather illustrate than interfere with each other."[20] It was not to be. Percival's opus prevailed and served as powerful precedent, while Gisborne's and Gregory's mainly gathered dust on library shelves.

There is little need to examine Percival's *Medical Ethics* in

Title page of Thomas Gisborne's An Enquiry into the Higher and Middle Classes of Society in Great Britain, Resulting from their Respective Stations, Professions, and Employments *(London: J. David, 1794). Chapt. 12 (pp. 383–426) deals with physicians' duties.* COURTESY OF THE NEW YORK PUBLIC LIBRARY.

great detail, since only the first two of its four chapters allude even remotely to matters of genuinely ethical reference. The first chapter, "Of Professional Conduct Relative to Hospitals," was the document prepared in response to the Trustee's request; it is almost uniformly profession-oriented. In its first article, it contains a statement that sets the tone of the chapter and that, as we shall see, was borrowed verbatim by the American Medical Association in 1847. The statement runs: "Physicians should study, also, in their deportment so to unite *tenderness* with *steadiness* and *condescension* with *authority*, as to inspire the minds of their patients with gratitude, respect, and confidence."[21] Judged in context, the statement was a well-intentioned rule of etiquette and practical counsel to the physician at the bedside; but it nevertheless stood in sharp contrast to Gisborne's formulations and strongly reflected the tradition of authority of the medical profession rather than primary concern for the patient's interests.

All of the thirty-one items in chapter 1, with one exception, are actually instructions and advice by professionals, the chief aim of which is to enhance the honor, dignity, and security of the profession itself. The exception—and it is only partial—is item three, which requires attention to the feelings and emotions of the patient. But it still reads more like a practical rule for the craftsman than a noble injunction to serve the patient more effectively. Item four, which is often cited for ethical implication, is a guild rule requiring that the patient usually be kept ignorant of his condition and is firmly in the profession's doctor-knows-best tradition.

The rest of chapter 1 is reminiscent, at times strikingly, of the content and intent of the "ethical" statutes of London's Royal College. All sorts of practical topics are covered: religious influences should be brought to bear as a matter of course, last wills and testaments should be encouraged, records should be kept, consultations should be encouraged, and doctors should never accuse each other of any sort of misdoing, however heinous, before the public. As for surgical operations, no spectators should be admitted without the surgeon's permission, the patient apparently having no voice in the matter. Item twenty-six says that when the patient is poor, the physician must exercise greater authority and greater condescension than when he is affluent.

Chapter 2 deals with "professional conduct in private or general practice," the reference being to patients who could pay for their care and were usually treated in their homes or in the physician's office. They should be accorded "attention, steadiness, and humanity" in lieu, presumably, of tenderness united with steadiness, and condescension with authority.[22] The greatest care must be taken to avoid "officious interference" in a case under the charge of another physician, the rules of professional etiquette being more complicated and more binding when patients are able to pay than when they are indigent.

The physician must not give free advice to patients who are able to pay but may attend members of the profession and clergymen, and their families, without charge. He must not use secret nostrums and must retire when senescence is at hand. But above all, he ". . . should guard against whatever may injure the general respectability of his profession."[23]

Chapter 3 governs the conduct of physicians toward apothecaries, and chapter 4 deals with medico-legal matters, including problems arising from the practice of settling offenses against personal honor by the use of pistols at twenty paces. Curiously, there is no mention of medical malpractice, the reason probably being that such actions were exceedingly rare in Britain at the time.

Percival's *Medical Ethics* served the needs of the Manchester

Infirmary very well indeed. While some of its injunctions are today archaic, many of its points are still valuable to the physician in practice. Its high-minded instructions to the physician to hold his personal conduct above reproach can hardly be questioned, even though their primary purpose was to protect the profession's reputation and authority. All things considered, the most pertinent objection to Percival's *Medical Ethics* is its title. A title that had been initially chosen by Percival was more suitable and less misleading: it was *Powers, Privileges, and Employments of the Faculty* [staff].

Percival's Ethics Crosses the Atlantic. The American Revolution was not long settled when a standing committee of the Association of Boston Physicians cited Percival's magnum opus, along with works by Benjamin Rush and John Gregory, the committee having been instructed in 1807 ". . . to propose a Code of Medical Police. . . . "[24] The result was a short document entitled "Boston Medical Police," which was accepted by the Association early in 1808. It contains nine brief sections dealing with physician-to-physician relations and admonishing members to uphold the good name of the profession. "Every man who enters a fraternity," says the document, "engages by a tacit compact not only to submit to the law, but to promote the honor and interest of the association so far as is consistent with morality and the general good of mankind."[25] But nowhere did the standing committee introduce the word ethics and the "tacit compact" mentioned was in no way comparable to the social contract of the political theorists of the Enlightenment, from Locke to Rousseau. Its closest analogue was the agreement between the medieval craftsman and his guild.

In 1823 the Medical Society of the State of New York adopted a "system of medical ethics" which, in its own words,

could ". . . be reduced to the form of a code of medical police. . . . "[26] The system contained five divisions and follows the form of "Boston Medical Police" rather closely. It
cites both Gregory and Percival but, unlike the Boston document, it contains a section entitled "Specifications of Medical Ethics in Practice," the emphasis being on sexual conduct
including, among other things, seduction of female patients,
and interference ". . . with matrimonial rights and the observance of a chaste and moral life."[27] With regard to the patient's right to know the truth, the New Yorkers said flatly
that it was not up to the physician to acquaint his patient with
the prospect of exitus. That disagreeable chore, they thought,
should be undertaken by a "Christian minister . . . or some
other authorized person."[28]

A few years after the New York code was drawn up, the
Medico-Chirurgical Society of Baltimore followed suit,
drawing freely on Percival and the New York statement. It
makes reference to the *Oath* attributed to the "father of physic"
and gives as its primary concern the desirability of maintain-
ing the profession's honor and dignity.[29] Unlike the earlier
codes, it contains a sternly worded section on the duties of
patients to their physicians, said to have been composed by
Benjamin Rush.[30]

Yet another publication that exerted a considerable influence on American medical organizations was Ryan's *A Manual of Medical Jurisprudence*, published in England in 1831 and
in Philadelphia the following year.[31] Ryan deals with ethics
in the tradition of John Caius, citing the *Moral and Penal Statutes* of London's Royal Society as published in 1830.[32] He also
refers to Percival's work but, for the most part, his concern
was with what would today be called forensic medicine.

All four statements (Boston's, New York's, Baltimore's, and
Ryan's) are immensely practical and, like Percival's proto-

type, they no doubt served a useful purpose among the physicians of the several cities. So probably did a much-quoted volume by Hooker[33] which, in nineteen chapters, conveys practical counsel about physician-to-physician behavior, and about the physician's proper demeanor in the presence of patients. But common to all five works is the hazy inference that if physician-to-physician etiquette is properly observed, good patient care inevitably follows and requires no special attention, as such.

Ryan's book appeared in the United States in 1832; Hooker's book was published in 1849. By that time the die was cast: the long-standing confusion between ground rules of etiquette, on the one hand, and ethical statements on the other, seemed to have become irreversible. Final proof came in 1847, when the newly formed American Medical Association adopted a lengthy code that faithfully followed Percival's line and that, in some respects, went beyond it. Meantime, a coherent law of malpractice was evolving in Britain and, like Percival's ethics, was transported more or less intact to the new United States, where American judges in the nineteenth century introduced modifications to suit the American purpose as they saw it.

The Shaping of an American Law of Malpractice. The interface between ethics and law is real and intermittently dynamic, and it is inviting confusion to deal with one without some consideration of the other. In theoretical terms ethics requires the fulfillment of a duty, while tort law, in a sense, concerns itself with repayment of a debt of some sort.[34] As for the medical guilds, it has already been shown that their spokesmen have traditionally placed the "ethical" duty of the physician to the profession itself above other professional duties. The profession's service ideal, or the duty owed by the physician to his patient, has been left largely to the physician's own conscience. On the rare occasions that organized medicine accused its members of unethical conduct, the offense was most frequently participation in group or contract medicine, fee-splitting, or consulting with unapproved practitioners. Charges against physicians by county or state medical societies alleging negligent, ignorant, or careless professional services to patients have been brought very rarely.

The law of malpractice requires a physician who has accidentally injured his patient to pay compensation for the injury to the patient, and thus, to liquidate the debt he has incurred. The apparent intent of malpractice law, unlike the medical profession's several codes of ethics, has been to protect the interests of both parties—doctor and patient—evenhandedly. It has, however, not always worked to so impartial an effect. But by applying tort law to the professions (medical and legal), public authority continued to serve notice that the professions' various codes of ethics were inadequate where prevention of injury, or compensation for injury attributable to negligence, were concerned.

As noted earlier, ancient Greek law, and probably early English common law as well, held the physician liable only if he injured his patient by specific intent; he was not legally liable for damages if injury to the patient resulted from ignorance or neglect. Fourteenth-century English judges, however, began to require physicians to treat their patients with diligence and to do all in their power to cure them. If, despite the physician's best efforts, the patient suffered injury or death, the physician was not liable. The new doctrine thus had the effect of protecting the patient from carelessness but not necessarily from ignorance or clumsiness. The physician, on the other hand, could not be expected to work miracles or be held absolutely liable to compensate for injury or death.

It was an individualistic test and it was, in time, replaced by what in legal language is an objective rule holding that a "defendant owes to those whom he may injure [accidentally] a duty to exercise due care—the care of an ordinarily prudent and careful man. The breach of that duty is actionable negligence."[35]

The common law developments from the time of Cavendish to the acceptance of the definition of negligence in terms of failure to exercise ordinary care have been dealt with by many legal historians[36] and are not easy for the non-lawyer to follow. As we have seen earlier, Bracton's writings in the thirteenth century convey a suggestion of liability for negligent conduct, and the suggestion was extended by English judges in the fourteenth century, especially with regard to physicians and veterinarians. Another stop on the way was Fitzherbert's "it is the duty of every artificer to exercise his art rightly and truly as he ought."[37] But the concept of negligence by omission or commission was not applied widely, apart from the field of professional malpractice, until the nineteenth century.

In early American colonial law, the conduct of physicians or would-be physicians was regulated after a fashion, the intent being to control substandard practitioners by requiring them to seek consultation (if available) whenever required, without intending to ". . . discourage any from all lawful use of their skills."[38] It was a requirement that reflected the geographic isolation of the Massachusetts colony at the time but that knew nothing of the law of malpractice based on negligence.

Title page of the first American edition (from the second English edition) of William Blackstone's Commentaries on the Laws of England. *The copy was once owned by Daniel Webster.* COURTESY OF BAKER LIBRARY, DARTMOUTH COLLEGE.

COMMENTARIES

ON THE

L A W S

O F

E N G L A N D.

IN FOUR BOOKS.

B Y

Sir WILLIAM BLACKSTONE, Knt.
ONE OF HIS MAJESTY's JUDGES OF THE COURT OF COMMON PLEAS.

RE-PRINTED from the BRITISH COPY,
PAGE for PAGE with the LAST EDITION.

A M E R I C A:

PRINTED for the SUBSCRIBERS,
By R O B E R T B E L L, at the late Union Library, in *Third-street*,
PHILADELPHIA. MDCCLXXI.

Common law concepts as they stood in the eighteenth century were, for the most part, transmitted to the thirteen colonies by Blackstone, whose *Commentaries on the Laws of England* appeared in 1765 and was reprinted from a second English edition in Philadelphia in 1771–1772. Copies went immediately to the governors of the colonies and to sixteen men who were to be among the framers of the Constitution. From that time to the end of the nineteenth century, Blackstone's *Commentaries* was the authority from which thousands of American law students received much of their instruction.[39]

Blackstone mentioned medical malpractice, apparently lifting a statement from a case decided in 1694:[40] ". . . mala praxis is a great misdemeanor and offence at common law, whether it be for curiosity and experiment, or by neglect."[41] He specified that *trespass on the case* was the proper remedy, not *trespass vi et armis*, thus indicating that malpractice is ordinarily a civil wrong, not a criminal one. The law of malpractice was approximately where Blackstone left it when the first American case of malpractice came to judgment in Connecticut.[42] Other cases accumulated slowly in the American legal record, but none plowed new legal ground.[43] The physician's status before the law was still somewhat ambiguous when a Massachusetts court, quoting England's Lord Chief Justice Hale, said that ". . . if a physician, licensed or not, gives a person a potion without any intent of doing him any bodily harm, but with the intent to cure . . . and contrary to the intent of the physician it kills him . . ." the physician is guilty of no crime.[44] Another American court, attempting

Title page of E. Maynwaring's Praxis Medicorum, *London, 1671. The work contains the earliest known use of the word* malpractice *(male-Practice to Maynwaring).* COURTESY OF THE NEW YORK ACADEMY OF MEDICINE LIBRARY.

Praxis Medicorum

ANTIQVA & NOVA:

THE
Ancient and Modern Practice
OF

P H Y S I C K

Examined, Stated, and Compared.

The Preparation and Cuftody of Medicines, as it was the Primitive Cuftom with the Princes and great Patrons of Phyfick, afferted, and proved to be the proper charge, and grand duty of every Phyfician fucceffively.

The new mode of Prefcribing, and Filing *Recipe's* with Apothecaries, manifefted an imprudent invention, and pernicious innovation.

Demonftrated from the treble Damage and Difadvantages that arife thence; to Phyfician, Patient, and the Medical Science.

With enforcing Arguments for a return, and general conformity to the Primitive Practice.

All Objections to the contrary, anfwered and fully cleared.

By *E. Maynwaring*, Doctor in Phyfick.

LONDON,

Printed by *J. M.* and are to be fold by *T. Archer* Bookfeller, under St. *Dunftan*'s Church in *Fleetftreet*, 1671.

to define malpractice a few years later, cited English precedents to the effect that ". . . nothing short of gross ignorance and want of skill will authorize a suit against a practicing physician."[45] This decision, as well as several English ones, was cited in the new nation's third malpractice case.[46] In 1853, two cases were decided, one in New Hampshire[47] and one in Pennsylvania,[48] in which English precedents were carefully summarized (one going back to Fitzherbert). They are noteworthy in that they made it unnecessary for later American jurists to cite the relevant English cases, and they established the English principle in American law that physicians are required to possess an ordinary degree of skill but not the highest degree possible; nor are they required to be warrantor or insurer.[49]

Blackstone had used the word tort to refer to suits (not founded on contracts) ". . . whereby a man claims satisfaction in damages for some injury to his person or property,"[50] but Kent, "The American Blackstone," hardly mentioned suits growing out of personal injury and did not use the word tort at all.[51] Nonetheless, the first book specifically on the law of torts (including medical malpractice) was by an American author.[52]

Until this time, malpractice law seemed to have been impartial, since it protected the physician from outlandish expectations and the patient from grossly substandard care. Both in Britain and in America, however, rapid industrialization brought a great increase in the number of lawsuits growing out of injury which, in turn, was due to a proliferation of industrial accidents.[53] The effect in both countries was a vast overloading of the courts, a burden that was so great in Britain as to produce radical reform of the legal system in 1873.[54] In the United States, the chief effect was a major restructuring of tort law focussing on a refined and more objective definition of fault and negligence.

It all grew out of nothing more momentous than a dogfight in Boston. In an effort to break up the fight, the owner of one of the dogs accidentally injured the owner of the other. In the lawsuit that followed, Massachusetts Justice Lemuel Shaw read into law a view contained in a then-current textbook. Its author, Professor Simon Greenleaf of Harvard, had written "The plaintiff must come prepared with evidence to show, either that the *intention* was unlawful, or that the defendant was in fault; for if the injury was unavoidable and the conduct of the defendant was free from blame, he will not be liable."[55] In accepting Greenleaf's concept, Shaw came down solidly on the concept of negligence defined as a failure to use that ". . . kind and degree of cure which prudent and cautious men would use." It was up to the injured party to prove that the individual or corporation that inflicted the injury was negligent, or "chargeable with some fault, negligence, carelessness, or want of prudence."[56] If negligence could not be established, the injured party received no compensation.

Negligence in this sense was well enough established by the eighteen-sixties for two American authors to write a book about it. Their definition of the standards by which physicians accused of malpractice are to be judged is, with small alteration, still valid.[57]

Shaw, more than any other American jurist, is credited with employing the common law to protect growing industry from the fiscal inconvenience of paying damages to workmen injured on the job.[58] The topic is a controversial one, but the facts are that by the turn of the century there was a mounting outcry at the injustice done by law to injured workmen and their families. The ultimate result was workmen's compensation laws,[59] which had the effect of relieving injured workmen of the necessity to go to court and, as plaintiffs, to establish fault in order to obtain compensation. Walter F.

Dodd, describing the conditions that brought about the passage of Workmen's Compensation laws, noted that

The employee's remedy for injury was by suit, but this remedy was ineffective because of the technical defense of the employer at common law and of the delay occasioned by the congested condition of the dockets of the courts. . . . If an employee obtained and collected a judgment, the probability was that half or more of the judgment recovered would go toward expenses and . . . contingent fees of an attorney. Many claims . . . were settled without suit, but the odds were so much in favor of the employer that there was little inducement toward . . . settlements, favorable to the employee. . . .[60]

One can with some justice apply Dodd's statement to the situation that prevailed until the mid-twentieth century with regard to medical malpractice law: for employee read patient, and for employer read physician.

The Locality Rule and Other Matters. As Shaw's decisions had the effect, rightly or wrongly, of protecting industry from paying damages to injured workers, so malpractice law began to be tailored so that it acted mostly in the physician's favor. One device that worked to this effect was the locality rule, which, like Massachusetts' statute of 1649, was a product of the frontier, where few doctors were likely to enter practice; of those that did, most were poorly trained. The rule said that professional performance had to measure up to that of physicians practicing in the same (later in the same or similar) communities, and not in cities where sophisticated facilities and highly trained physicians were likely to be found. It originated in a textbook on malpractice law written in 1860[61] and was read into law by Justice Stafford of the Supreme Court of Kansas in 1870.[62] The standard of professional performance prevailing in any community required expert testimony which, in many instances, was difficult or impossible for the plaintiff (but rarely for the defendant) to obtain. This, and other factors, led to the development of what has been called a conspiracy of silence, a professional protective device that shielded physicians in malpractice actions much as nineteenth-century common law rules had protected employers in industry. It was not merely that physicians were almost routinely reluctant to testify in court against each other. There was, in addition, overt action by some medical organizations to abet the conspiracy.[63] In one instance, a county medical society proposed to expel one of its members for unethical conduct because he had given testimony against another doctor in a judicial proceeding.[64]

The locality rule, which was never adopted in Britain, remained in force in American law for many decades. As time passed it came to be applied to general practitioners, rather than to certified specialists who must, in most states, measure up to a national standard of professional performance laid down by their own specialty organizations.[65]

The slow retreat of the locality rule in the American law of malpractice, which began before World War II, was accelerated by a decision in 1968,[66] which abolished it in Massachusetts. Other states have followed suit, although the rule is not yet totally extinct. Its abolition in many states may reasonably be viewed as part and parcel of a liberalizing trend that tends to improve the patient-plaintiff's chances of winning malpractice actions. So also do two other common law devices that have their roots in earlier times and that are now being invoked by plaintiff's lawyers with increasing frequency in malpractice actions.

The first of them is *res ipsa loquitur* (the thing speaks for itself), a doctrine that is said (probably wrongly) to go back to Roman law. The Latin phrase was used as a last-ditch tactic by Cicero, whose client, Titus Annius Milo, was on trial for murder. Cicero's tactic was unsuccessful,[67] but eighteen hundred years later an English jurist, Frederick Pollock, introduced the same Latin phrase into English common law under different circumstances. It seems that an innocent passerby in Liverpool was injured when a barrel of flour rolled off a raised loading dock and struck him on the shoulder. The suit was against the owner of the flour firm, who in fact was not on the premises at the time of the accident. But Pollock reasoned that barrels of flour do not fall on innocent pedestrians unless there is negligence which, beyond the occurrence of the event itself, need not therefore be proved.[68] The rule entered American malpractice law soon after the turn of the century, the case being one in which a surgeon accidentally left a strip of gauze in a patient's peritoneal cavity.[69] Subsequent cases involved injuries sustained by patients while under general anesthesia, the reasoning being that common knowledge indicates that such accidents do not occur unless someone—usually a doctor or nurse—is negligent. Expert testimony is therefore unnecessary.[70] Legal authorities are divided on the ultimate effect that freer application of the *res ipsa loquitur* doctrine is likely to have. The conservative view is that the doctrine should be narrowly interpreted and applied only in situations where the layman's common sense tells him unequivocally that someone was negligent.[71] The opposing view is that rules governing the applicability of the rule should be greatly liberalized, mainly in order to overcome ". . . the notorious unwillingness of members of the medical profession to testify against one another."[72]

Probably more important, in reducing the advantage malpractice law based on the fault principle formerly gave to the physician, is the doctrine of informed consent, which is still being defined in American courts.[73] The term is of recent origin,[74] but its roots reach far back into English common law. It is of particular interest in that it is an unusually clear example of the gradual passage of a well-established ethical principle into law. Blackstone cited Magna Carta as the basis for the right of personal security and said that "both the lip and limbs of a man are of such high value in the estimation of the law of England that it pardons even homicide if committed *se defendendo* or in order to preserve them."[75] And in book three, he says "The least touching of another's person wilfully, or in anger, is a battery; for the law cannot draw the line between different degrees of violence and therefore totally prohibits the first and lowest stage of it; every man's person being sacred and no other having a right to meddle with it, in any the slightest manner."[76] An early American decision carried the principle into American common law[77] and thence it entered American textbooks on the law of torts.[78]

The general principle was taken up in 1859 by John Stuart Mill, that most loyal of Benthamites, who in *On Liberty* says "That the only purpose for which power can be rightfully exercised over any member of a civilized community, against his will, is to prevent harm to others. His own good, either physical or moral, is not a significant warrant. . . . Over himself, over his own body and mind, the individual is sovereign."[79]

In the United States, the principle of sovereignty over one's person was the focus of an Illinois case decided in 1905, in which the principle was applied in a successful action against a physician who performed a hysterectomy without obtaining the patient's consent.[80] About the same time, a physician in Minnesota was required to pay a patient $14,322.50, an enormous sum for the day, under similar circumstances.[81]

Most present-day courts go back no further than a decision by Benjamin Cardozo, then sitting on the Court of Appeals of New York, in which he said that "Every human being of adult years and sound mind has a right to determine what shall be done with his own body; and a surgeon who performs an operation without his patient's consent commits an assault for which he is liable in damages."[82]

Informed consent as a legal doctrine has been in a state of rapid evolution in American law since 1960.[83] The general effect of the developments to date is to protect the patient's sovereign right to decide what is to be done to him or her and to establish the legal principle that if medical procedures are applied without his or her fully informed consent and there is injury as a result, the physician is at fault. In addition, if the physician proceeds without informed consent, he or she may be charged with a criminal offense (battery) as well as a civil one.

The English common law of malpractice had thus, in principle at least, been transported almost intact to this side of the Atlantic by the third quarter of the nineteenth century and had begun to undergo modest transformation to meet specific American needs. In the United States, as in Britain, its actual effect was usually to protect the practicing physician from financial loss attributable to malpractice, very much as certain specific features of tort law protected American industry from financial loss attributable to industrial accident. Early in the twentieth century, however, workmen's compensation laws began to replace the no liability without fault principle where industrial accidents were concerned and imposed in its stead a form of absolute liability on American industrial employers. American malpractice law, however, continued to favor the practicing physician until after World War II, when a distinct movement in the direction of favoring the plaintiff came to be evident. One action to this effect was the gradual abolition of the nineteenth-century locality rule; another was to apply increasingly liberal interpretations of *res ipsa loquitur;* the third, still very much in progress, is a movement that broadens the application of informed consent.

Beginning in the sixties, a so-called "malpractice crisis" was one result of these changes, but it may well be more precise to label it an ethical crisis of sorts. At the very least, ethics and the common law of malpractice are playing separate but strongly related roles. In the process, it is coming to be understood, within and without the medical profession, that the ethical physician can no longer be defined as one who does not advertise, split fees, or consult with naturopaths.

6 · Codes and Principles of Ethics of the American Medical Association, 1847–1957

By the middle of the nineteenth century, or a bit later, most American states had a recognizable law of medical malpractice, based mainly on English precedents. The American medical profession was in the process of organizing itself partly, if not primarily, to establish its supremacy over other types of healers and to raise standards of medical education.

Two men of medicine came over on the *Mayflower*. One of them, Dr. Samuel Fuller, stayed; the other, Dr. Giles Heale, want back with the ship when it returned in April 1621.[1] But there was nothing recognizable as a medical profession in the colonies until well along in the next century. Even then, medical organizations were small and limited to the major population centers. There was a medical society in Boston, which in the 1730s began to proclaim the need to regulate the practice of medicine in the public interest.[2] New York and Philadelphia followed soon after, and the first state medical society was established in New Jersey in 1776.[3] By the time of the Revolution, or soon after, the medical profession in the new nation was beginning to establish itself, and was beginning to do battle against irregulars and quacks. By the 1830s almost all states had medical societies and all but three had licensing laws constructed in favor of the regular practitioners of medicine.[4] But then, for reasons that are not altogether clear, reaction set in. There was, for one thing, a vast proliferation of proprietary schools, which granted medical degrees for a price after very short periods of indifferent training. Then as now, regular physicians were accused, when attacking their ill-educated competitors and the schools that turned them out, of arrogance, bigotry, and covert efforts to establish monopoly. In addition, the Jacksonian era (1828–1836) brought with it an upsurge of antipathy toward special privileges of all sorts, and in this climate most state medical licensing laws were swept away. By 1845 ten states had repealed their medical licensing laws and the rest had either never enacted such a law or exercised only token control over licensure.[5]

Britain was also experiencing a similar but not identical counterreaction. Parliament had sought, in the sixteenth century, to protect the public from medical imposters and to enhance the access to competent medical professionals by legislation in favor of London's Royal College of Physicians. But the College seems ". . . to have considered chiefly the personal advantage of [its] members or the corporate advance of the body."[6] The final result was the Medical Act of 1858, which abolished rigid distinctions between physician, surgeon, and apothecary, and created a nominally homogenous medical profession in Britain.

There was, however, never a professional organization in the colonies and the later United States that was comparable in status and authority to London's Royal College of Physicians. But the College was, in the eyes of men of medicine in the United States, a powerful prototype and a highly desirable one in many respects. In the United States the regular medical profession, having established itself reasonably firmly at least on the eastern seaboard by the eighteen thirties, was by the forties an embattled minority fighting for its life. As a defense measure, among other reasons, it sought security in unified organization and in what Konold calls "ethical controls."[7]

The Founding of the American Medical Association, 1847–1957. The real beginning was in 1845, when Alden March and Nathan Smith Davis, both members of New York State Medical Society, discussed the desirability of convening a national medical convention.[8] Davis then introduced a resolution for the purpose, and the convention was held in New York in May 1846. The convention, firmly dominated by Davis, first resolved "to institute a National Medical Association for the protection of their [the profession's] interests, for the maintenance of their honour and respectability, for the advancement of their knowledge, and the extension of their usefulness,"[9] presumably in that order. Its second resolution was for the construction of a plan of organization, to be reported in May 1847. Resolutions three, four, and five had to do with encouraging and refining regular medical education.

Resolution six had this to say: *"Resolved,* that it is expedient that the Medical Profession in the United States should be governed by the same [i.e., a common] code of Medical Ethics and that a Committee of Seven be appointed to report a code for that purpose at a meeting to be held at Philadelphia on the first Wednesday of May 1847."[10]

The committee of seven, composed of members from Pennsylvania, Delaware, Rhode Island, New York, and

Georgia, got down to business with Isaac Hays of Philadelphia carrying most of the burden. John Bell, also of Pennsylvania and like Hays a graduate of the University of Pennsylvania, wrote the introduction to the code that was presented to the new association, now called the American Medical Association, and was accepted by it without modification in 1847.

At the outset, Bell's introductory statement struck a lofty quasi-academic tone by saying that medical ethics was a branch of general ethics and therefore rested on religion and morality. Borrowing from the language of formal philosophy, he went on to say that the duties and rights of the physician ". . . are identical with Medical Deontology." After making the customary obeisance to Hippocrates, he got down to the basic purpose of the proposed code and, for that matter, of the new association itself. The physician must advise public authority as well as individuals and has a right to be "attentively and respectfully" listened to. Then came the matter of the superiority of the "regularly initiated physician," with his "learning and impartial observations, accumulated for thousands of years, over interloping empirics." The regular physician must combat apothecaries who sell quack medicines and nostrums and those "members of the sacred profession," i.e., the clergy, who, like the press, encourage, "aid, and abet the enormities of quackery." Bell then called by inference for legal control of quackery: the law, he said is ". . . silent and, of course, inoperative in the cases of both fraud and poisoning so extensively carried on by the host of quacks who infest the land. . . . By union alone can medical men hope to sustain the dignity and extend the usefulness of their profession. . . . Greatly increased influence for the entire body of the profession will be acquired by a union for the purposes of common benefit and the common good; while to its members individually will be insured a more pleasant and harmonious intercourse one with another. . . .[11] Physicians are, he says, "trustees of science and almoners of benevolence and charity." As if his point were not already driven home, he requires physicians to ". . . use increasing vigilance to prevent the introduction into their body of those who have not been prepared by a suitably preparatory moral and intellectual training. . . . We are under the strongest ethical obligations to preserve the character which has been awarded by the most learned men and best judges of human nature to the members of the medical profession, for general and extensive knowledge, great liberality and dignity of sentiment, and prompt effusions of beneficence."[12]

Bell thus sounded the theme of the welfare of the guild and the demand for monopoly repeatedly and forcefully, but usually in pious disguise. The new AMA needed a strong organizational document that could be presented to the public as an instrument of high moral purposes, that would give the AMA's leaders firm control over its members (especially those who failed to follow the party line absolutely), and would insure the monopoly of the regulars. The Code of 1847 met all these requirements admirably.

In a note appended to Bell's introduction, Isaac Hays acknowledged the committee's indebtedness to prior codes and especially to Percival's, whose actual words were preserved whenever they served the committee's purposes. A few sections were attributed to "the late Dr. Rush" and others.[13]

The Code of 1847 is in three chapters. Chapter I ("Of the Duties of Physicians to their Patients and of the Obligations of Patients to their Physicians"), sets a highly paternalistic tone and includes Percival's instruction concerning uniting tenderness with firmness and condescension with authority.[14] Physicians are also told not to make unnecessary visits or to gossip about their patients; nor should they follow the example

Isaac Hays (1796–1879) of Philadelphia, who opened the proceedings at Philadelphia (5 May 1847) that resulted in the formation of the American Medical Association. A month later he presented the report of the Committee on Medical Ethics, citing William Percival and Benjamin Rush as important sources. The Code was adopted as recommended and stood virtually unchanged for over half a century.
COURTESY OF THE NEW YORK ACADEMY OF MEDICINE LIBRARY.

of the empirics by making gloomy statements about patients who are not seriously ill in order to make their professional services look more remarkable. On the other hand, physicians ought not to abandon patients who are incurably diseased and, in difficult or protracted cases, consultation should be unhesitatingly sought.

Article 2 of Chapter I, entitled "Obligations of Patients to their Physician" and usually attributed to Benjamin Rush, was generally judged by those laymen who saw it to be extraordinarily arrogant and demanding. It required patients to select only regular physicians and to place total trust in their judgment, to obey them promptly and implicitly, and to ". . . entertain a just and enduring sense of value of the services rendered; . . . for these are of such a character that no mere pecuniary acknowledgment can repay or cancel them."[15]

Chapter II deals with physician-to-physician etiquette, but with little else. It is professionally unbecoming to advertise or to patent discoveries or to fail to uphold the honor and dignity of the guild in any way. Elaborate rules for consultation are set out in Article 4, the first of which precludes any form of professional relationship with irregular practitioners. To avoid misunderstanding, a specific definition is included: ". . . no one can be considered a regular practitioner, or a fit associate in consultation, where practice is based on an exclusive dogma to the rejection of the accumulated experience of the profession, and of the aids actually furnished by anatomy, physiology, pathology, and organic chemistry."[16] Other instructions concerning consultation are almost ritualistic in their detail: they set out who should speak first, when a medical umpire is required, and when a physician supporting a minority view should "politely and consistently" retire from further involvement. Finally, there is an admonition to protect the character and reputation of the

physician in attendance as far as is consistent with "a con-
scientious regard for truth." Along the same line, Article 6
requires that differences between physicians be resolved by a
court-medical in secret and never publicly.

Chapter III deals with the profession's duties to the public,
and vice versa. As good citizens, physicians must be ready to
advise public authorities on medical matters, including giving
testimony in court, but should receive "a proper honorar-
ium" for such services. Most important, physicians should
expose quackery whenever they encounter it and should en-
lighten the public as to the ". . . injuries sustained by the
unwary from the devices and pretensions of artful empirics
and imposters."[17]

The Code of 1847 closes with stern instructions to the public
to give physicians their utmost consideration and respect, and
to ". . . entertain a just appreciation of medical qualifications: to make a proper discrimination between true science
and the assumptions of ignorance and empiricm," and to encourage regular medical education as much as possible.[18]

The Code was thus mainly, if not quite exclusively,
profession-oriented, as were its predecessor codes, including
the *Oath* attributed to Hippocrates, the ethical and penal statutes of London's Royal College of Physicians, and Percival's
rules for the staff of the Manchester Infirmary. The AMA's
Code refers from time to time to an ideal of service that focuses by inference on the needs and rights of the patient. Such
references are, however, often linked with profession-oriented commands. For example, Chapter I, Article 1, Section
1 says: "a physician should not only be ever ready to obey
the calls of the sick, but his mind ought also to be imbued
with the greatness of his mission. . . ."[19] Along the same line,
Chapter II, Article 1, Section 1 instructs the physician "to be
ever vigilant for the welfare of the community" where public

health measures are concerned,[20] but Section 4 brings us back to the Code's main theme by sternly requiring the physician to expose relentlessly quacks and quackery and those apothecaries who sell secret remedies and nostrums.

At its eighth annual meeting, the AMA required all state and county constituents to adopt the Code of 1847 as a condition for membership in the National organization.[21] In the following year, the president of the association acknowledged that the line of demarcation between regular and irregular physician was often not very distinct, even to the professional eye; but he spoke glowingly of the association's great crusade ". . . against the evils which had been usurping the sacred places of the profession." He then called for wide distribution of the Code, especially to young men about to enter on the study of medicine.[22] Presumably as a consequence, the association reprinted the Code every year in its *Transactions*, from 1857 (volume 10) until the *Transactions* was replaced by the *Journal* in 1883, and irregularly thereafter. At no time did the AMA attempt to hold its Code and statutes secret, as had London's Royal College for the first several centuries of its existence. To the contrary, the leaders of the AMA seem to have thought that wide distribution of the Code would convince the layman of its selflessness and noble intent. That it was moved by other concerns, however, was implicit in the comments of one of its early presidents, who said that "Eschewing politics, proposing to control medicine alone and seeking no aid from State or Church, we should become a law unto ourselves, or rather act above all law save the divine, since it is quite certain that we alone must protect the honor of the medical profession."[23] To which he might well have added its growing monopoly in the provision of personal health services. It is not altogether certain, over a century later, to whom such pompous and bombastic utterances were directed. Since most were contained in presidents' addresses to the membership, their usual purpose must have been to induce members to close ranks against the threat of unorthodox healers. At the time, few laymen had occasion to read the AMA's *Transactions*, and its presidents' addresses, although sometimes mentioned in editorials in the lay press, rarely made the headlines. The importance of such utterances, in retrospect, probably resides mainly in the insight they provide into the profession's own view of itself: it did indeed come to place itself above "all law save the divine."

The Revisions of 1903 and 1912. The AMA's Code of 1847 proved to be remarkably durable and, judging from the record, served the association's needs very well indeed. There were, however, occasional objections, the most notable being that brought by the New York State Medical Society in 1882. The New York Society rejected the AMA's Code and promulgated its own, the reason being that the New Yorkers considered the prohibition of consultation with irregular practitioners to be arbitrary and unduly restrictive. They preferred a provision that allowed the regulars to consult with all "legally qualified practitioners" in the State of New York, a designation that included some whom the AMA considered beyond the pale.[24] One spokesman for the AMA said the action by the New Yorkers was treasonable, and that ". . . in the defection of New York . . . we may find our medical Sumter."[25] A lay commentator from New York took a dim view of the AMA's rigid stand, accusing it of ". . . narrow spirit of exclusiveness and of individual rights which bears far too near relationship to that of the medical guild." He advised the regular medical profession ". . . to accept the fact that an irregular physician is not necessarily and *ex officio* a knave;" and that ". . . if a knave he is not thereby and consequently a fool"[26]

But the AMA was not to be moved by such appeals, nor by the editor of the *New York Medical Journal*, who in 1892 demanded that the AMA abolish its Code of Ethics entirely.[27] Still, dissatisfaction with the Code of 1847, most of it centering on the flat prohibition of consultation with any but members in good standing of the AMA and constituent societies, would not die. Finally, key members of the New York State Medical Association themselves revised the AMA's Code of 1847 and presented their version for consideration by the AMA's then new House of Delegates in 1902.[28] The president appointed a special committee to consider the revision and make recommendations at the next annual meeting. After considerable maneuvering at the annual meeting in 1902 at New Orleans, a revision entitled "Principles of Medical Ethics," allegedly prepared the night before by William H. Welch,[29] was adopted.

The change in the title was highly significant: the association's guide to ethical conduct was no longer a code that could and would be enforced; it was now merely advisory.[30] Gone was the haughty, authoritarian wording in Chapter I, Article (now Section) 1. Gone without a trace was the old Code's arrogant and self-serving instructions to patients on their numerous obligations to the physician. But much more important, the prohibition of consultation with irregular physicians was no longer absolute. Article 4 of Chapter II in the old code said flatly that no irregular was ". . . a fit associate in consultation" and, as noted earlier, defined an irregular as one untrained in anatomy, physiology, pathology, and organic chemistry. The Principles of 1903 now said simply that physicians could not ". . . designate their practice as based on an exclusive dogma or sectarian system of medicine,"[31] but that "the broadest dictates of humanity should be obeyed by physicians whenever and wherever their services are needed to meet the emergencies of disease or accident."[32]

Otherwise, the Principles of 1903 stood firm: regular physicians should join the local, stae, and national professional organization, must not advertise, must not split fees or steal patients from other physicians, and must cooperate fully with public authority where public health measures were concerned.[33] The intent of the revision of 1903, and the substitution of *principles* for *code*, seems to have been to eliminate the basis for the criticism brought by the New Yorkers and others. But it also had the effect of placing disciplinary action mainly on the shoulders of state and county societies.

The result was not altogether satisfactory, and in 1911 the Association's Judicary Council began to take back the reins of disciplinary authority and to complete a second revision of the Code. The revision, adopted in 1912,[34] was still entitled "Principles of Medical Ethics," and was far less offensively worded than the original Code. The injunctions against advertising and fee-splitting were unmodified and a vaguely worded condemnation of contract practice appeared for the first time. In a concluding statement, the authors of the revision of 1912 said outright what had only been implied in the two earlier revisions: ". . . these principles," they wrote, "are primarily for the good of the public," the inescapable inference being that the good of the organized profession and the good of the public were synonymous.[35]

It may be recalled that between 1912 and 1919, the AMA moved temporarily away from its traditional political conservatism and participated in drafting a model health insurance bill that it rejected vehemently a few years later. In 1920 and 1922 the House of Delegates passed resolutions which placed organized medicine in implacable opposition to federal health legislation if it had to do with personal health services.[36] Since the 1920s, the AMA has fought a losing battle in its efforts to keep the federal government out of the provision of personal health services to individuals. Throughout this period, the Judicial Council has continued the difficult business of categorizing as ethical or unethical an array of topics that, by their nature, usually raise no genuinely ethical question at all.[37]

Richard Cabot on Medical Ethics. Even so, the matter of medical ethics still occasionally attracted attention and discerning comment. One of the most remarkable of them came from Boston's Richard C. Cabot, who at the time, was persona non grata to the AMA because of his interest in certain types of contract practice. Cabot got to the heart of the matter by warning the profession that ". . . the problem of contract practice brings out a peculiar feature of medical ethics: that in endeavoring to protect their group interests against certain "unfair" practices the physicians are likely at any moment to discover that they are acting against the public interest. . . ."[38] He then went on to say that ". . . the strongest force for ethical advance has been, in my experience, the intimate contact with other medical men better than themselves, whereby by "osmosis", nobler habits of thought and action seep across from teacher to pupil, from chief to interne, from colleague to colleague, without a word spoken on the subject."[39] His reference was to that grandest of Boston medical traditions, the clinical rôle model whose behavior at the bedside was impeccably and effortlessly ethical but who, half a century after Cabot's article was published, is fast disappearing.

In characteristically trenchant language, Cabot went on to deplore the absence of opportunities in medical schools to discuss ethical topics and, anticipating the views of many present-day observers, said that ". . . [students] want to know about *euthanasia*, that ancient and reliable novelty, that dependable stimulant of readers' interest in the news of the day, the shopworn discussion which the newspapers trick out afresh each year in August when politics are dull and there is dearth of copy. Students want to hear the pros and cons of birth control, of state medicine, of abortion, of the use of bread pills, of medical advertising . . . and [of] many other matters."[40]

Cabot's much neglected commentary partly explains an often-noted paradox: there is a striking discrepancy between the public actions and statements of organized medicine on the one hand, and the noble service to patients unhesitatingly rendered by many individual physicians, on the other. As Cabot indicates, their care of patients is in large measure determined by the examples set by some, if not by all, of their clinical teachers, while the AMA's Codes and Statements of Principles are no more than their guides to professional etiquette and their ground rules for conduct within the guild.

What may not inappropriately be labelled the Boston ethical tradition as passed on by a succession of deeply committed clinical teachers to many classes of medical students and house officers in the Boston area until the passage of Medicare and Medicaid laws significantly altered the circumstances under which bedside teaching is carried out in teaching hospitals. Rôle models of the Cabot type, who linked patient-centered medical ethics with the best that scientific medicine had to offer, are today all too rare. But the memory of one of them still lingers in American academic circles, and his example and writing still serve now and then to convey the essence of the physician's ethical obligation. He was Frances Weld Peabody, Director of the Thorndike Memorial Laboratory at the Boston City Hospital and one of Harvard's professors of medicine. The importance, in terms of crystallization of the ethical obligation of the physician to his patient, of Peabody's small opus *The Care of the Patient*[41] can scarcely be overstated. Most often quoted is his final sentence: ". . . the secret of the care of the patient is in caring for the patient," implicit in which is a sense of the patient-oriented ethic. Much closer to the point is a formulation that is very often overlooked: "The treatment of a disease may be entirely impersonal [i.e., scientific]: the care of a patient must be completely personal. The significance of the intimate personal relationship between physician and patient cannot be too strongly emphasized, for in an extraordinarily large number of cases *both diagnosis and treatment are directly dependent on it.* . . ."[42]

In this short passage Peabody captured the essence of the two elements of the physician's ethical obligation: he must know his professional business, and he must trouble to know the patient well enough to draw conclusions, jointly with the patient, as to what actions are indeed in the patient's best interests. That done, the physician then places these actions above all other considerations within the professional relationship. Most important, he must not fall into the delusion that application of the most sophisticated scientific knowledge, on the one hand, and caring for the patient, on the other hand, are mutually exclusive.

Most of the writings of Boston's great clinicians, that were intimately concerned with medical ethics, were published before 1930, yet to this day they remain remarkably relevant. Mentioned earlier were Cabot's allusions to the hunger of medical students for lectures on such topics as euthanasia and abortion. Comparable is Peabody's observation that the older practitioners of his day were critical of young medical graduates because ". . . they are too 'scientific' and do not know how to take care of patients."[43] Then there is his view that "death is not the worst thing in the world, and to help a man to a happy and useful career may be more of a service than the saving of life."[44]

What is most relevant in the present context is that the Boston tradition incorporated the teaching of medical ethics by powerful example, and that the virtual disappearance of the clinical role model since the nineteen-fifties has left a void in American medical education that has not yet been filled. Lectures and seminars in formal ethics, usually adapted to the medical purpose, have not, unfortunately, wholly compensated for the disappearance of the role model.

The AMA's Ten Principles: Beginning of Decline. The teaching of medical ethics by the role-model method was in sharp contrast to stands taken by the AMA, as spokesman for the American medical profession, especially in the late thirties and after. In 1938, the AMA attempted to penalize members for joining a group practice organization, alleging that such action was unethical. At the time, the power of organized medicine over its members was almost absolute. It was, in fact, extraordinarily difficult to practice medicine anywhere in the country without being a member in good standing of county, state, and national medical associations. As a result of its action against members who chose to join group practice organizations, the Attorney General of the United States brought suit against the AMA, alleging violation of the Sherman Antitrust law. After a prolonged trial, the decision went against the AMA which, from that time forward, could no longer overtly interfere with the formation of group practice organizations.[45] It did, however, continue to oppose federal health care proposals. It gave carte blanche in 1948 to a public relations firm to mount a campaign in its name in opposition to national health insurance. The tactic seemed to be successful, since a proposal to establish national health insurance was defeated.[46] But for the AMA the victory was decidedly pyrrhic: to many laymen and physicians the campaign had been scurrilous and was evidence that the AMA could not be trusted to act in the public interest if, in its view, its own prerogatives were under threat.[47] In retrospect, it seems likely that the years 1948 and 1949 saw the AMA pass the peak of its power, prestige, and prosperity. The events of those years undoubtedly brought the association's Principles of Medical Ethics, and its politicies in general, under critical review within and without its membership. One result was that the Judicial Council once again began to consider revising the association's Principles of Ethics.

In June 1949, the Council presented a revision of the Principles of Medical Ethics as they had stood, with minor amendments, since 1912.[48] The revision of 1949 said by implication that individual physicians may practice in clinics or groups but are still subject, as individuals, to "the principles of ethics herein elaborated."[49] The revision also said that physicians' incomes should come from fee-for-service practice and that the physician "should not accept additional compensation, secretly or openly, directly or indirectly, from any other source."[50] There matters rested for a few years, until the Judicial Council came forward in 1955 with a reorganization of the Principles of 1949, which divided them into three categories.[51] Part 1, which bore the title "The Domain of Medical Ethics," contained two sections that spoke of service to humanity (quoting the *Oath* attributed to Hippocrates) and the physicians' "inflexible standards of personal honor." Twenty-nine following sections then dealt with organizational and professional matters and matters of professional decorum taken from the revision of 1949. Part 2, "The Domain of Manners," covered instructions having to do mostly with relations with other physicians, especially when in consultation. Its title was, for the most part, accurate: the concern was indeed with manners or etiquette between physicians. Part 3 dealt mainly with organizational matters.

The proposed revision of 1955 was not accepted by the House of Delegates, and in 1956 the Judicial Council, working with the Council on Constitution and By-laws, took the radical step of reducing the Principles of Medical Ethics to a brief preamble followed by ten short sections. To justify its action, it cited the examples of the U.S. Constitution, the Ten Commandments, and the *Oath* of Hippocrates. The new Ten Principles, said the Council, omitted no "fundamental ethical concept."[52] After much discussion and revision of revisions, the Ten Principles were recommended to the House of Delegates and were finally accepted by the body in June 1957.[53] The new rules required that the physician serve humanity with respect for the dignity of man and the rights of patients. Physicians must also keep up with medical advances and must not base their practice on exclusive dogma or sectarian systems, nor voluntarily associate with those who do; they must expose "illegal or unethical conduct of fellow members of the profession;" and must neither abandon nor solicit patients. Principle six vaguely discouraged what was earlier called contract practice, and Principle seven repeated an eralier rule that the physician should ". . . limit the source of his professional income to medical services actually rendered by him to his patients." Principles eight, nine, and ten continued to encourage the use of consultants when needed, the protection of confidence, and cooperation with public authority "in activities . . . [for] the improvement of the health and welfare of the individual and the community."

To supplement the new Ten Principles, the Judicial Council brought out a guide that was considerably longer than the Codes and Principles of 1949 and earlier. In a historical introduction, the Council said that the "earliest written code of ethical principles for medical practice was conceived by the Babylonians around 2500 B.C."[54] The reference, presumably, is to the laws of Hammurabi of about 1790 B.C., which contained nine statutes that regulated physicians' fees and prescribed penalties for certain untoward therapeutic results: But none of the statutes dealt even remotely with ethical matters. The Council next pointed to the *Oath* of Hippocrates as "an expression of ideal conduct for physicians," a view that ignores both the content and the context of the *Oath* attributed to Hippocrates. The Council's guide then expanded on the familiar principles of practice and procedure that the AMA, following the precedents set by John Caius and Thomas Percival, has usually included in its Code and later Principles of Medical Ethics. The Council's guide runs to sixty-eight pages and contains much that is undoubtedly useful to officials of medical societies and to physicians concerned with medical etiquette. In addition, it touches on its several uses of the word *ethical* and on the relation between ethics and law; it also alludes to the physician's ethical obligations, but in terms that are too general to be meaningful.

On 22 July 1980, the AMA's House of Delegates reduced its Ten Principles of Medical Ethics, adopted in 1957, to seven and, in so doing, broke very considerably with its conservative past. The move was not altogether spontaneous. For one thing, the Federal Trade Commission had charged that the AMA was acting illegally in forbidding its members to advertise, thus suppressing competition among doctors.[55] In addition, the AMA was the target of numerous lawsuits brought by chiropractors, charging that Principle three of the Ten Principles of 1957[56] represented a conspiracy designed to deny them the right to practice.

The new code, in response to FTC pressure, makes no

mention of advertising or solicitation of patients. Principle five of the new code says that physicians should ". . . obtain consultation and use the talents of other health professionals when indicated." This broadly permissive provision replaces Principle three of the 1957 code and does not rule out consultation with chiropractors or other unorthodox healers.

Much more significant are changes in language and in tone in the new Seven Principles. In the preamble, physicians are required to recognize a responsibility to patients, society, other health professionals, and to self. Along the same line, the new Principle four requires the physician to respect the rights of patients, of colleagues, and of other health profession. Prior codes, from the *Oath* attributed to Hippocrates to Percival's code to the several AMA codes, have all been guild- or profession-oriented, the patient's interests being left to inference or ignored altogether.

The new Seven Principles thus comes closer than prior codes to recognizing the obligation that is unique to the medical profession: to place the patient's interests before all else within the professional relationship. The new document somewhat redundantly requires the physician to "respect the law" (Principle three), "to deal honestly with patients and colleagues," and to "safeguard patient confidences within the constraints of law" (Principles three and four). Redundancy enters because in the climate of today it is hardly necessary to remind the profession of its obligation to show respect for the law. The requirement that the physician deal honestly with patients, taken literally, means that the physician may not, under any circumstances, withhold information from the patient. It is doubtful, however, that the authors of the new Seven Principles had such a strict reading in mind. In any event, debate within the profession centering on the desirability of withholding information when it seems to be in the patient's interest to do so is likely to continue for a long time to come.

The reminder that the physician has obligations to society as well as to the individual patient is not new and conveys nothing more than the sense that all citizens, whatever their expertise, must when appropriate make their services available in the service of the society of which they are a part. The new code fails to spell out, in so many words, the physician's social contract (or covenant), which binds him to respect his patient-centered ethic in exchange for special social and economic privileges. But the principle is more nearly implicit in the new code than in any of the previous ones.

For reasons that are unconvincing, Robert M. Veatch considers the "patient benefit emphasis" to be paternalistic, and criticizes the committee report that accompanied the new Seven Principles for saying that the principles are "primarily for the benefit and protection of the patient."[57] He draws the conclusion that the statement implies that "doctor knows best," and that "benefit and protection" are to be defined solely by physicians themselves. Actually, the statement is innocent of such implication and, as Veatch himself notes later, the committee report "recognizes on both theoretical and practical grounds the importance of the lay person in determining what is ethical in the relationship between lay person and professional."[58]

What seems to be lacking in the views of Veatch and moral philosophers of similar persuasion is comprehension of the essential ingredients of the doctor-patient relationship if the patient's interests are to be well served. The routine, almost reflex, denunciation of the relationship as paternalistic usually suggests that logical and systematic discussion of the physician's basic ethical obligation to the patient is unwelcome.

One can discourse learnedly on ethical obligations to society, as AMA leaders seem to have done in the past, as a means of avoiding altogether mention of the more binding patient-centered obligation. Such practice brings to mind Peter Caw's warning that ". . . along with rational convictions about moral behavior there must always go, in some form or other, an identification with the particular person . . . who [is] affected by this behavior, *if the situation is to be morally alive.*"[59]

It is extremely important, in the present climate, to recognize the new Seven Principles for what they are: a beginning departure from the guild mentality to which organized medicine has been bound from the Hippocratic period to our own. The new concern for the patient is not, per se, paternalistic. There are times when the doctor does indeed know best, even though he or she may not impose a decision; ultimate choice is incontestably the patient's. Veatch calls for a vaguely defined "social covenant between society and the profession."[60] But he and other serious critics of organized medicine should now be prepared to give the devil his due: for all its past transgressions, organized medicine appears to be ready to move with the times. Judith Swazey's view is more tenable: the social contract type of relationship should be preserved, with the difference that all aspects of it must become fully visible and acceptable to both parties.[61]

Paradoxically, doctrinaire hostility to organized medicine may well be as serious a barrier to such an outcome as professional intransigence once was. The medical profession must, after all ". . . both preserve its essential functions and serve the insistent needs of society."[62]

7 · The Future: Ethical Profession or Politicized Industry?

Medicine, in theory the prototypical profession, may at long last be approaching ethical maturity, if one defines maturity in terms of placing the patient before the brotherhood or guild. That it has taken the calling nearly two millennia to begin the approach is extraordinary enough. Yet more extraordinary is the divergence through the centuries between the belief and behavior of many individual physicians, on the one hand, and the pronouncements and political or quasi-political actions of the organizations speaking for physicians, on the other hand.

The concern for a patient-centered principle of medical ethics has become general only since the end of World War II, and was in large part initiated by forces outside the medical profession. The most important external force may be characterized as social and political in nature, acting mainly through the medium of legal precedents collectively known as the law of malpractice. An internal force of lesser proportions began to be felt when certain relatively recent technological developments came into general use and brought the patient's inherent right to refuse treatment, and the alleged right to die with dignity, into sharper focus. As Robert Nisbet so aptly puts it, ". . . the oldest of ethical issues can become activated by technologic success in medicine."[1]

The Law of Malpractice in Transition and Chaos. The convention that all presentations dealing with medical matters should begin with usually irrelevant, and often inaccurate, references to the Hippocratic Corpus has mercifully begun to die out. But it is still appropriate when the matter under consideration is the liability of physicians for harm to patients growing out of substandard practice. In a treatise written before the beginning of the Christian era, Hippocrates is said to have complained that medicine was the only art ". . . which our states have made subject to no penalty save that of dishonor. . . ."[2]

With a few exceptions, the situation described by Hippocrates remained unchanged until the fourteenth century, when English public authority had come to regard the efforts of the medical guild (or guilds) to police its own ranks as inadequate, and its willingness to penalize physicians guilty of careless or otherwise substandard practice as less than convincing. There ensued a series of contests between the guild and the courts that has endured to our own time. In the United States, organized medicine, by the adroit use of various manuevers and political devices, managed to preserve many special prerogatives of the profession almost intact, until the middle of the present century.[3] Until that time, patients who had sustained injury as a result of substandard medical practice as defined by law stood small chance of winning compensation by resort to the courts. Malpractice law served, in effect, as a highly effective protective device for physicians. One indication of the degree to which physicians were pro-

tected was the size of premiums for malpractice insurance; until
1950 or thereabouts, premiums for most practitioners were
very low, seldom exceeding one hundred dollars per year.
Today annual premiums routinely run fifty to a hundred times
that sum, and even higher for certain high-risk specialists.

In retrospect, the handwriting was on the wall in the United
States when the locality rule began to be weakened, when rules
for the application of *res ipsa loquitur* (the fact speaks for itself) were liberalized, and especially when the right to be left
alone began to be cited by the courts in actions brought by
injured patients against physicians and hospitals.[4] From such
origins has emerged, among other precedents, a continuing
progression from simple, ill-defined consent to informed consent. The end is not yet in sight. Since the early seventies,
courts have been struggling with such slippery topics as standards of disclosure, the acceptable meaning of informed, and
methods of proving that the patient did or did not understand the information provided by the physician.[5] Although
few firm legal rules have as yet emerged, it is increasingly
clear that the authority of the medical profession is no longer
accepted as absolute in many, and probably in most, courts.
What is emerging is the solid principle that although it is the
physician's obligation to discuss in full, and to recommend
(and justify) a specific course of action, the final decision must
rest with the patient, who must, by some acceptable standard, have been fully informed. One court has gone even
further by setting up its own standard of professional performance and rejecting that offered by medical experts.[6]

This extraordinary, and potentially dangerous, precedent
seems at present to be an isolated one. It calls to mind Plato's
dire predictions of the damage to be expected when professional standards are established by untutored laymen.[7] There
may, in addition, be a beginning awareness that an effective

doctor-patient relationship may become impossible if the legal definition of informed consent turns out to be too rigid and unrealistically narrow. Also to be queried are the ethical and legal problems that will inevitably arise when patients begin to gain admission to health care systems by conversing with a computer.[8]

The present situation concerning malpractice law and the evolution of its legal definition and standards is so rapidly transitional as to be occasionally chaotic. This was unquestionably brought about in part by the belated reaction of courts and the public to the advantage given to the physician in malpractice actions when Lemuel Shaw's fault principle and the locality rule remained in full force. There is also the fact that developments since World War II represent in some measure a quickening of the ordinarily slow passage of ethical principles into law within the ethics-law continuum. Activity at the ethics-law interface was never more dynamic. Predictably, however, while professional negligence may be reducible to some very low incidence, it can never be abolished altogether; neither can so-called statistical accident. It is clear, therefore, that some form of after-the-fact system of compensation for medical injury will remain for the foreseeable future. But what form will it take?

Toward Strict Liability. In an incisive article written thirty years ago, Charles Gregory took a long look at things to come in tort law. Why, he asked ". . . should not the courts either adhere to the clear-cut legal principles of Shaw's day, leaving any departure from them to the legislature, or cut clean away from them with open acknowledgement of a modern theory of absolute liability without fault . . . if they are going to effect the change anyway, without benefit of legislation."[9] This was written well before the advent of the so-called malpractice crisis of the nineteen-seventies. Gregory recognized the major defects in the system of malpractice law as it then existed (and as it still exists, but in more liberal form). Since then, litigation based on personal injury due to medical malpractice has grown by leaps and bounds, and the chief defects in the system have become painfully apparent. As exemplified in malpractice cases that come to trial, the most glaring defects are apparently irremediable: they are the inordinate amount of time required from injury to final settlement (four to six years being not uncommon), and the relatively small percentage of the total award that finally reaches the injured party, owing in no small part to fees paid to plaintiff's attorneys under the contingent fee system and to the ". . . extraordinarily high transaction costs of the present system."[10] In a recent case decided in Brooklyn, a jury awarded a five-year-old plaintiff over $29.2 million some four years after the injury occurred.[11] Probably, as newspaper accounts routinely fail to convey, the amount may well be reduced on appeal, which will require an additional one or two years. Even so, the plaintiff's attorney will, under court rules of New York's Second Department, receive from 25 to 33 percent of the final award and the patient considerably less than half of it. The case exemplifies the necessity, under present conditions, to raise the total award to astronomical levels in order that the amount received by the plaintiff be adequate.

The transition from a fault to a no-fault (strict liability) system for medical malpractice may well require many years but, in the end, the course to which Gregory made reference in his query seems likely to win out: medical treatment will one day be classed, in William L. Prosser's words, as ". . . a hazardous enterprise . . . which must pay its way and make good the damage inflicted."[12]

There are today many advocates of various versions of the no-fault system (especially for products but also for automobile accidents and medical malpractice) on the American scene. But objections are many, and serious. In New Zealand, however, an attempt is under way to overcome the defects in the tort system based on the fault principle by abolishing it altogether. In the New Zealand experiment, the conviction is that government itself should provide protection at a reasonable level against economic loss from accidental injury to the person, regardless of the actual cause. In a report that preceded legislative action, Mr. Justice Sir Owen Woodhouse sounded an ethical note by citing as the first reason for an effective system for compensating citizens injured in accidents ". . . *the civilized reasons of humanity.*"[13] He also said that "the injured worker himself has a moral claim . . ." and that "compensation for injury is a community responsibility."[14]

The details of the New Zealand scheme, and its advantages and disadvantages, are beyond the present scope. It represents, however, the first complete rejection, in a common law country, of a legal system that began in medieval precedents and became vastly overloaded by a great upsurge of industrial accidents prior to the turn of the twentieth century and that, in our own time, is seriously defective. Although the New Zealand approach is not likely to be acceptable in the United States, what Mr. Justice Woodhouse called ". . . the civilized reasons of humanity" also influence American jurists very prominently.

It should be noted that in socialist New Zealand, the primary obligation of the physician is to the patient, as it is in the United States and Britain. In the collectivist Soviet Union, however, it is quite otherwise. A recent article by I. I. Kosarev says that the physician's oath in the U.S.S.R., as revised in 1971, lists three requisites in order of importance.

First is adhrence to communist ideals, and possession of Marxist-Leninist convictions; second is participation in continuing education and attainment of high professional skill and knowledge; and third is personal intellectual development and "culture." Unlike the loose observance of codes of ethics in the bourgeois countries, Soviet physicians, the author notes, are under constant observation, and deviation from Soviet principles is publicized and critically evaluated both by the medical community and by the public. Such deviations (or "antagonistic contradictions"), Kosarev adds in chilling terms, are promptly resolved. But the author also notes that medical practice requires both scientific competence and a sense of responsibility toward patients; he is sharply critical of practices in Western nations where medicine is turned ". . . into commerce, and . . . everything not related to fee-for-service is thrust into the background."[15]

The Right to Die Serenely. Next to the debate about standards of physician performance, including informed consent, truthtelling, etc., the most vigorous controversy where the ethics-law continuum is concerned has to do with the process of dying. Within that debate, death is seen as more or less imminent and treatment, if any, is to ensure a peaceful and serene process to exitus, precisely as it probably was in ancient Greece and as it certainly was in ancient Rome. The debate is a derivative of the right to be left alone (and thus, to refuse treatment). Eighteenth- and nineteenth-century English physicians, if they could survey the American scene in the late twentieth century, would probably wonder what all the fuss is about. Some of the most prominent among them left considerable literature on the subject. William Munk, for example, counselled that once the patient is definitely and clearly not long for this life, ". . . we dismiss all thought of prolongation of life, and our efforts are limited to the relief of . . . pain, exhaustion, dyspnea, spasm, and the like. . . ."[16] John Ferriar would let the patient die in peace and would avoid ". . . unavailing attempts to stimulate the dissolving system, from the idle vanity of prolonging the flutter of the pulse for a few more vibrations. . . ."[17] Opium was the drug of chief resort, the dosage ". . . to be governed solely by the effect and relief afforded."[18] Henry Holland was even more direct. The use of opium in patients who are dying ". . . is not to be measured timidly by tables of doses, but by fulfillment of the purpose for which it is given."[19] All would avoid consciously hastening death, but tacitly recognized that the line between making the dying patient comfortable, and actually inducing his death, may be very thin indeed.

The practice of withholding treatment in hopelessly ill patients in order to permit early exitus has probably been a real but carefully concealed matter among physicians of all nationalities for centuries, and the introduction of antibiotics and life-sustaining cardiorespiratory techniques has intensified the right-to-die dilemma. As a consequence, legislators in fifteen states have been persuaded to pass so-called right-to-die, or natural death acts,[20] actions that have been greatly influenced by two much-publicized cases.[21,22] In one of them the court briefly commented on medical ethics: "We find that the current state of medical ethical opinion largely supports the right of the terminally ill to refuse treatment and to allow the natural process of death to run its course."[23]

It is still quite another matter to hasten death by prescribing or administering fatal doses of drugs, or by other positive, intentional steps.[24] The framing of legislation that will permit such action (now labelled homicide) is a matter of immense, and perhaps insurmountable, difficulty. Stanford H. Kadish has summed it up by noting that killing a person violates his most basic right, while letting him die does not.[25] It seems clear, however, that withdrawal of life supports such as respirators and artificial kidneys in patients who are terminally ill is, under certain rules and circumstances, sanctioned by law in a growing number of states. The reasoning, legal and clerical, seems to be that in such patients the process of dying is already well established and withdrawal of artificial support systems is no more than allowing the process to run its natural course. But the addition of a lethal agent, even in patients who are apparently terminal, is not now sanctioned by law.

When or if the courts or legislatures will act to permit termination of life by administering a lethal agent is uncertain, and for good reason. The possibilities of abuse of such a statute or precedent are all too obvious. The reluctance of courts and legislatures, in the absence of foolproof means of preventing abuse, is well taken.

The Physician and the Moral Philosopher. The future of malpractice law, and precedents and statutes concerning the right to die serenely, seem in broad principle to be already determined. The whole, as already noted, is in large measure the result of pressure to translate ethical principles into case law or statute, and the chief impetus has come from forces outside the medical profession.

There is abundant evidence, however, that some segments of the medical profession are intensely interested in medical ethics and, as a consequence, are engaged in continuing dialogue with moral philosophers. Results to date are mixed, largely owing to the fact that the two groups have as yet only fragments of language in common. Ian B. Thompson says that in Britain ". . . the reaction of the medical profession to most contemporary philosophy is contemptuous for its pedantic irrelevance . . .", because it seems to take refuge in ". . . so-phisticated discussion of the trivia of the language of morals," thus avoiding the "concrete dilemmas of individuals. . . ."[26] Part of the problem is that codes of medical etiquette, in to-day's intellectual and social environments, can no longer masquerade as codes of ethics; confusion between the two, as has been shown, has been characteristic of the medical profession for centuries. In addition, both philosopher and physician have developed their own traditions of exclusivity and professional authority, sometimes appearing as paternal-ism. The resulting clashes and calculated misperceptions were recently displayed with refreshing candor in an exchange be-tween Cheryl Noble (philosopher-lawyer), Peter Singer (phi-losopher), Jerry Avorn (physician), and others. Noble's main points (methods of moral thought are not the same as moral wisdom, "one could easily infer that the mastery of theoreti-cal ethics is a prerequisite for justice,") carry the day.[27]

None of which, however, alters the fact that dialogues be-tween physician and philosopher may sooner or later bring several critically important topics into full view. The medical profession has never developed a forum within its structure that is suitable for the systematic discussion of such items and has, as a consequence, been handicapped in many ways through the centuries. The present dialogue between philos-opher and physician may represent the beginning of such a mechanism. In its absence, what must, lacking a better term, be called a philosophy of medicine remains an empty, hap-hazard framework. The beginning needs now to be carried forward in such a way that virtually every physician compre-hends the critical importance of a coherent philosophy of medicine within which at least three areas of primary impor-tance may be continuously under consideration: first, the ba-sic nature of medicine and how its members see themselves;

second, the patient-centered ethical principle; and third, medicine's tradition of authority as it pertains to the doctor-patient relationship, and especially as it occurs in the doctor-doctor exchange.

What Is Medicine? Is medicine hard science, behavioral science, social science, art, trade, or some sort of humanism? This question is far and away the most important agenda item for a philosophy of medicine as the second millennium A.D. draws to a close. On the answer depend such basic considerations as how the physician should be educated, what his or her fundamental obligations are, and even how he or she thinks.

For centuries, physicians have at times defined their calling in terms designed to assist in the struggle against competing groups such as the apothecaries, and later the osteopaths, homeopaths, and chiropractors. It is worth noting that Article IV of Chapter II in the original Code of Ethics of the AMA defined "irregular" healers as those who were untrained in anatomy, physiology, pathology, and organic chemistry.[28]

When the AMA's original Code of Ethics was constructed (1847), many members in good standing were virtually untrained in the sciences specified in the code or in the natural sciences (biology, chemistry, and physics), none of which were well-established subjects in American colleges and universities. As the "hard," or natural, sciences began to emerge as legitimate disciplines, however, the question of medicine's identity seemed settled. In the sweeping enthusiasm for the natural sciences in the last quarter of the nineteenth century, it was assumed that medicine in its entirety must be based on them and that, ultimately, all medical questions would soon be answerable in terms of biology, chemistry, or physics. It was recognized that many fragments of the natural sciences had no known relevance to medicine but, on the assumption that every such detail, however remote, *might* one day relate to medical problems, the conviction was that aspirants for medicine must be exposed to each of the natural sciences in depth. In the late nineteenth century, a few prominent men of medicine, mostly British, warned against such simplistic reasoning. William Henry Gull, M.D., F.R.S.; for example, said that "No one can hope, even as the sciences now stand and much less as they shall further advance, to obtain a foremost knowledge of them and of medicine at the same time." He also warned against assuming that science was so far advanced that "a complete and satisfactory theory of man" was in the offing. It was rash, he thought, to believe that medicine might one day "have no separate existence" from what he called the collateral sciences. "But this consummation," he added, "appears to be as yet far distant and must be so acknowledged."[29] Thomas Henry Huxley, F.R.S., a contemporary, vigorously campaigned for the inclusion of the natural sciences in school and university curriculums, but noted that the introduction of botany and zoology as separate elements in curriculums preparing students for medicine also introduced "a large mass of matter which is very valuable no doubt in itself, but to the medical student is entirely irrelevant."[30] In his address *On University Education*, delivered at Johns Hopkins University on 12 September 1876, Huxley urged President Gilman and his colleagues, unsuccessfully as it turned out, to adopt a realistic definition of the purposes of medicine as a guide to planning premedical and medical curriculums. "What is the object of medical education?" he wanted to know. Then, answering his own question, he said:

It is to enable the practitioner, on the one hand, to prevent disease by his own knowledge of hygiene; on the other hand, to divine its nature and to alleviate or cure it by his knowledge of pathology, therapeutics, and practical medicine. That is his business in life and if he has not a thorough and practical knowledge of the conditions of health . . . of the meaning of symptoms, and of the uses of medicines . . . he is incompetent even if he were the best anatomist, or physiologist or chemist, that ever took a gold medal or won a prize certificate.[31]

Huxley also spoke out against adding to medical education ". . . one iota or tittle beyond what is absolutely necessary," and against training all medical students as if they were to become laboratory scientists.[32]

The Hopkins model for medical education, later to become standard in the United States, was constructed on the assumption that medicine rests, or should rest, almost solely on a foundation of natural science. The timely warnings of Gull, Huxley, Acland, and several other English educators, whose counsel was sought by Gilman of Hopkins, are dismissed today on the ground that they applied only when the natural sciences were still young and uncomplicated. The more considered view, however, is that the English educators were remarkably perceptive and prescient, and that their views and reservations have come to be more applicable in our time than they were in their own.

Overall looms a giant paradox: in its century of greatest technological advance, the medical profession has become increasingly confused as to its intellectual and social identity. The single-minded theme on which the Hopkins curricular model was constructed was a mixed blessing, although, in view of the enthusiasm for the natural sciences in the last quarter of the nineteenth century, it was perhaps inevitable. It persists as the second millennium A.D. draws to a close for a mixture of reasons, most of them no more than tactical. Despite overhelming evidence that medicine is a free-standing and very complex enterprise, hardliners still persist. Ludwig

Eichna, for example, recently went so far as to put his prejudice in peremptory terms: "Biological science is medicine. Teach that."[33]

Medicine is not a single science in the narrow sense of the word. It is, in Ronald Munson's terms, ". . . an autonomous discipline with its own aims, contraints, and framework of basic commitments."[34] That it draws heavily on the natural sciences, and increasingly on the behavioral and social sciences, there can be no doubt. This being the case one might call it a poly- or suprascience or, in George L. Engel's phrase, "a system-oriented biopsychosocial model."[35] Whatever name is applied to it, medicine is unique and is not, in its entirety, comparable to any one science. Its most compelling difference is that it, unlike bioscience, chemistry, and physics, possesses ". . . an inherently moral aspect."[36] Wherever possible, it applies principles and techniques drawn from individual sciences to prevent or alleviate disease in the human being, but when lack of knowledge makes this impossible, medicine relies ". . . upon empirical rules that are validated (at least partially) by practical success."[37] The practice of medicine is thus inescapably practical; at times it is an empirical pursuit. To apply these adjectives to a so-called hard or pure science (e.g., physics), however, is to risk giving offense to hard or pure scientists. To them, these are the characteristics of a trade, not a science. However this may be, the fascination with positivism may be easing somewhat, and Edmund D. Pellegrino's view that ". . . medicine is the most scientific of the humanities and the most humane of the sciences" has increasing pertinence. The felicitous phrase, however, is not likely to extract us from real and pressing difficulties concerning a sufficiently valid definition of medicine. More penetrating and conclusive is the longer treatment of the matter by Pellegrino and David C. Thomasma.[38]

From such considerations, it becomes clear that medicine as an essential enterprise can be defined only in its own special terms; none of the individual sciences or trades or other vocations are actually comparable. If the medical calling, and all that is in it, is considered lacking in intellectual respectability by the pure scientist, the problem resides mostly in that individual's own ignorance or prejudice or both. It would, in fact, be occasionally disastrous if the physician approached clinical problems employing the methods of the theoretical physicist, biologist, or chemist.

Invidious comparisons between the practice of medicine and various sciences thus are usually inaccurate and inappropriate. In the heyday of physics, after Sputnik was launched,[39] those who sought careers in physics were compared by Harvard's G. Holton to mountain climbers aspiring to attain the most rarefied intellectual climate; all others were classed with the "eternal lowlander, the stolid farmer, the congenital subway rider. . . ."[40] Such analogies hardly need to be taken seriously. The professional practitioner, whether physician or physicist, need feel inferior only if he or she does not know his or her professional business or carries out professional assignments negligently or carelessly, or (with reference to the discipline) unethically.

Medicine's Ethical Imperative. The physician, as physician, has a special moral obligation to his patient. This is one of the points—perhaps the chief one—that differentiates him or her from pure scientists and from many other professionals. The point is, however, a matter for debate among philosophers. K. Danner Clouser, for example, says that ". . . in medical ethics we are really working with the same moral roles that we acknowledge in other areas of life," but he makes allowances for "certain elaborations in deference to the special facts and relationships of medicine."[41] Alan H. Goldman seems to be in agreement, but goes on to define professions as groups applying ". . . a specialized body of knowledge in the service of important interests of a clientele."[42] Gerald J. Postema, however, speaks out strongly against abandonment of the concept of a special professional role, and objects to the view that ". . . the duties and responsibilities of a professional are no different from those of any lay person facing a similar moral problem." He sees nothing morally objectionable in what he calls the "exclusionary character of professional morality."[43] In Martin L. Norton's view, the discussion has to do with ". . . the moral responsibility to our patient, to society, and to those who, in their despair, seek our aid—not our responsibility to our profession, or to our personal convenience or aggrandizement. This does not imply self-deprivation but rather a return to idealism, to that truly fiduciary relationship which places the client/patient first and foremost in the time-honored traditions of service, duty, and honor."[44]

Those not familiar with the intricacies of moral philosophy may have the disquieting feeling that all four of these highly qualified authors are, in effect, saying somewhat the same thing. But Norton comes closest to providing a working definition (and a jog to the conscience of the professional) that is least likely to be misunderstood. The distinctions he specifies are fundamental; without them, principles of medical ethics become too theoretical to be of significant moment in the day-to-day life of the practicing physician.

The Tradition of Professional Authority. One element among medicine's traditions that often (and insidiously) opposes understanding of the basic medical ethic is the very strong tradition of authority. It is not usually recognized that the tradition of authority possesses two points of references: one has to do with the doctor-patient relationship, the other with doctor-to-doctor etiquette and intellectual rapport. In a very important sense, the latter may be far more detrimental to standards of professional performance than the former.

Enough has already been said to make clear that the doctor's authority over his patient is today far from absolute. The doctor knows best concept is mindlessly embraced by few doctors trained in the last decade, and by a decreasing number of laymen. The principle of informed consent has so altered the pattern of transmission of information from physician to patient that medicine's tradition of authority, physician over patient, is rapidly undergoing massive alteration. Yet Molière's seventeenth-century caricature of the doctor in an authoritarian pose is occasionally, though rarely, appropriate in our own enlightened day. In *Le Malade Imaginaire*, Dr. Purgon views a patient's refusal to carry out doctor's orders as "a crime of high treason against the profession which cannot be sufficiently punished."[45] Considerably more fanciful than Molière's witty contrivance is the view of a recent author, who compared medicine to patriarchal religion and advanced the astonishing principle that medicine, like the Church, figuratively sanctions the "marriage of man to man in spiritual brotherhood under the appearance of celibate brotherhood." Medicine, she continued, ". . . has historically been another example of a male homo-relational union."[46]

Such fantasies might safely be ignored were it not for the fact that they tend to draw the attention of physician and philosopher from other, more critical, aspects of medicine's tradition of authority. Probably the most critical is that which induces the practicing physician to accept the views of medical "authorities" without question. The mechanisms by which some physicians come to be regarded by other physicians as authorities is not altogether clear, but frequent presentations at medical meetings, as well as numerous contributions to medical journals and a favorable lay press, are contributing factors. The important point, however, is that once a physician is regarded as an authority, his descriptions of diseases and his recommendations for diagnosis and treatment are likely to be accepted uncritically, often by both physician and layman. Such recommendations, if faulty, may exact a considerable toll in money and in lives before they lose favor, usually quietly, in the ranks of the profession. Cases in point are many. The routine removal of tonsils and adenoids during childhood is one of the most flagrant, having been accepted by most physicians for half a century. It is now on the way to being almost totally discredited. Other, less spectacular, items are certain other surgical procedures, the indiscriminate administration of antibiotics for such ailments as head colds, and the uncritical administration of addictive drugs such as barbiturates and other hypnotics. All such items enter medical practice backed by medical authority of some sort and, once in use, are very difficult to eliminate, no matter how weighty the evidence in opposition. In a sense, they may be considered to represent malpractice, not by a single physician but by the entire profession.

Physicians, steeped in science since the Flexner revolution of 1910, should above all have learned to demand and appraise evidence before adopting untried techniques and procedures. The tradition of authority within medical education and the profession in general has, however, worked against such a practice. Perhaps the most valuable result of the physician-philosopher debate now going on in many institutions is that it tends to nudge the physician toward questioning, in clinical settings, the time-honored intraprofessional tradition of authority. That questioning, in lieu of blind acceptance of authority, is a very fundamental part of the physician's ethical obligation to the patient. The "rigorous, systematic ethical analysis" of the moral philosopher should be directed not only at the tradition of the physician's authority over the patient; it should be brought to bear with even greater force and inspiration against the tradition of physician's authority over physician.

Conclusion

The medical profession, and perhaps other service professions, stand at last on the treshold of becoming ethical. Over the past two millennia, the medical calling has approached the matter of its ethical *raison d'être* very timidly indeed, and has generally been more at ease with the minimalism of the Hippocratic admonition to do no harm than with the more positive ethical principles that are implicit in Amos 5:23, in Luke 12:48, in the writings of Scribonius Largus, and more massively in the literature of the Englightenment.

Two processes in our own century, the one philosophical and legal, and the other scientific and technological, have converged to bring the medical profession to an activity of self-appraisal that is unique in its long history.

The philosophic and legal force began to be visible late in the nineteenth century; by the middle of the twentieth, it was of major magnitude. Its chief consequence is the vigorous translation of ethical precepts into legal precedent. By such means our system of malpractice law is in process of major overhaul. If the result has at times been chaotic, the general direction and intent are hardly questionable.

Technological advances have brought to the fore the patient's rights in other connections. One is the classic doctor's dillemma as portrayed in Shaw's play of the same title: how to allocate scarce and expensive resources among equally needy patients. A second result is the increase in the frequency of cases in which the patient's right to die serenely is central.

It is possible to predict with some confidence how these several forces and actions will wind up. In the area of malpractice law, some form of strict liability is virtually inevitable. With regard to death with dignity, the practice of withdrawing life-support measures from hopelessly ill patients seems certain to gain general social and legal acceptance. Still very much at issue is the matter of positive action (e.g., administration of lethal doses of analgesic or hypnotic drugs).

Far less predictable is the future position and conduct of the medical profession, although its cooperation with lay authorities in preventing substandard medical practice (and thus reducing medical injury to patients) is already well established. Much more fundamental is the sober recognition of the profession's deeply embedded tradition of authority. From that tradition flow many more or less ineffective features of medical practice which, even though conscientiously applied, are not only unproved but may also injure the patient, sometimes fatally. Less directly, but as important or more so, is the contribution that slavish acceptance of authority by physicians makes to the rapidly rising costs of health care. This unhappy result of the tradition of authority consists not only of unnecessary treatment, but also of uncritical use of costly adjuncts such as hospitalization in lieu of (often preferable) ambulatory care, and an intricate battery of excess laboratory studies. In bringing health care costs under control the physician is the key, despite the fact that hospital costs have escalated more rapidly in the last decade than physicians' fees. But the principle of larger-fee-for-less-service, especially since the passage of the Medicare-Medicaid amendments, is a time bomb of sorts, ticking away under the profession's independence.

Underlying the entire medical edifice, and actually emphasizing some of its most undesirable features, is the prevailing system of education for medicine. That system, despite recent modifications, is still based on a distorted view of the physician's social role and ethical obligation, and on the anachronistic view that medicine is solely bioscience. As it stands, the system from its early premedical stages strongly transmits and reinforces medicine's tradition of authority.

It is safe to conclude that no matter how progressive the medical profession becomes socially and politically, its best efforts at becoming truly ethical and optimally effective are not likely to succeed unless it overhauls its system of education at all levels. This in turn requires *intelligent and precise definition of the scientific and humanistic bases for the practice of medicine.*

Two millennia of mistaken emphases with regard to the essential *raison d'être* of the medical profession are surely enough. The profession's opportunity in the free world is, first, to clarify its basic ethical position by placing the patient—not the profession—at the center of its considerations. Second, but virtually parallel, is a firm and unfettered appraisal of the profession's ancient tradition of authority. Key to both pursuits is the redesign of our system of education for medicine.

Failure to respond to what may well be the last call must someday result in some sort of redefinition of what Scribonius called *professio*, and a reduction of the physician at least to the role of the craftsman as in the Golden Age of Greece.

In the final analysis, the professions' privileges have to be deserved and frequently renewed. None are eternal.

Notes

INTRODUCTION

1. Chester Burns, "Medical History and Medical Humanities," in *Teaching the History of Medicine at a Medical Center*, ed. Jerome Bylebel (Baltimore: Johns Hopkins University Press, 1982), pp. 35–36.

2. The original proposal was to create a system for compulsory federal health insurance and federal support of medical education. It was introduced as Social Security Act Amendment of 1943, Unified National Social Insurance (S. 1161, 78th Congress, first session, 1943). It was reintroduced several times, the last being on 5 January 1949. The AMA employed a California public relations firm, Whittaker and Baxter, to mount its attack on the proposal, which was represented as creeping socialism, a threat to the American way of life, and contrary to the American tradition. The proposal never came to a vote, but within a few years, new proposals to establish federally backed health insurance for the aged and indigent began to appear. The final proposal (Medicare-Medicaid) became law on 30 July 1965.

3. Carleton B. Chapman, "On the Teaching of the Science of Medicine," *Clin. Res. Proc.* 4:161–165, September 1956, p. 162.

CHAPTER I

1. The activities and methods of the healer in prehistoric and ancient human societies are discussed by Guido Majno, *The Healing Hand: Man and Wound in the Ancient World* (New York: Commonwealth Fund, 1975), especially pp. 1–28.

2. This is a date ordinarily given. See D. C. Darlington, *The Evolution of Man and Society* (New York: Simon and Schuster, 1969), pp. 100–102.

The evolution of cuneiform representation from a sort of three-dimensional form dating from c. 8000 B.C. to the undimensional representation in use from 3000 B.C. well into the first millennium B.C. has been virtually established by Denise Schmandt-Basserat (*Sci. American* 238:50–89, June 1978). See also A. Leo Oppenheim *Ancient Mesopotamia: Portait of a Dead Civilization* (Chicago: University of Chicago Press, 1964), pp. 49–50.

3. Henry Maine, *Ancient Law* (New York: Dutton, 1972), pp. 70–82: ". . . the penal law of ancient communities is . . . the law of Wrongs or, to use the English word, of Torts."

4. As opposed to the ascending thesis, in which original power rests with the people. See Walter Ullmann, *Medieval Political Thought* (Harmondsworth: Penguin Books, 1975), pp. 12–13.

5. Samuel Noah Kramer, "Sumerian Historiography," *Israel Exploration J.* 3:217–232 (1953).

6. Samuel Noah Kramer, *History Begins at Sumer* (New York: Doubleday Anchor Books, 1959), pp. 104–113. See also Kramer's *The Sumerians: Their History, Culture and Character* (Chicago: University of Chicago Press, 1963), pp. 123–126.

7. James B. Pritchard, ed., *The Ancient Near East: A New Anthology of Texts and Pictures* (Princeton: Princeton University Press, 1975), vol. 2, p. 31.

8. Francis Rue Steele, "The Code of Lipit-Ishtar," *Amer. J. Archaeol.*, 52:425–443 (1948).

9. Pritchard, *The Ancient Near East*, vol. 2, pp. 12–34.

10. Pritchard, *The Ancient Near East*, vol. 1, pp. 133–138. The legal theory that the instrument that causes the death, in this case the ox, must be destroyed came to be known by the Latin term *deodandum* (given to God) and lingered in English common law until the nineteenth century. See generally Jacob B. Finkelstein, "The Goring Ox: Some Historical Perspectives on Deodands," *Temple Law Quart.* 46:169–290 (1973).

11. There is still disagreement about Hammurabi's dates. The dates used for his reign, and for those of the earlier rulers whose laws are cited, are those proposed by J. A. Brinkman in Oppenheim, *Ancient Mesopotamia*, pp. 335–347.

12. G. R. Driver and John C. Miles, *The Babylonian Laws* (Oxford: Clarendon Press, 1955), vol. 2, pp. 79–81. A shekel of silver weighed 8.5 grams (Majno, *The Healing Hand*, p. 476, no. 56).

13. Samuel P. Asper and Fuad Sami Haddad, "History of Medical Ethics, Contemporary Arab World," *Encyclopedia of Bioethics* (New York: Free Press, 1978), vol. 2, p. 888. The authors place the date of the laws at 2250 B.C., which is about half a millennium too early.

14. Driver and Miles, *The Babylonian Laws*, vol. 2, p. 13 and p. 97.

15. Kramer, *The Sumerians*, pp. 123–126.

16. Driver and Miles, *The Babylonian Laws*, vol. 2, p. 251.

17. Edith K. Ritter, "Magical-Expert (= ASIPU) and Physician (= ASU): Notes on Two Complementary Professions," in *Babylonian Medicine*, Oriental Inst., Univ. Chicago, Assyriological Studies, No. 16 (Chicago: University of Chicago Press, 1962), pp. 299–321.

18. Morris Jastrow, "Babylonian-Assyrian Medicine," *Ann. Hist. Med.* 1:231–257 (1917).

19. The best-known definition is that so grimly stated in Exodus (21:23–25): ". . . thou shalt give life for life, eye for eye, tooth for tooth, hand for hand, foot for foot, burning for burning, wound for wound, stripe for stripe." The legal principle, however, is far more ancient than the Old Testament.

20. G. R. Driver and J. C. Miles, *The Assyrian Laws* (Oxford: Clarendon Press, 1935), p. 385, statute 8. The accent in the Assyrian law that has come down is on family law, but the principle of compensation also figures prominently.

21. E. Neufeld, *The Hittite Laws* (London: Luzac, 1951), p. 4; statute 10.

22. The greatest of them, "the great religious geniuses of the eighth, seventh, and sixth centuries B.C.," were Amos, Hosea, Isaiah, Micah, Zephaniah, and Jeremiah. See Abram L. Sachar, *A History of the Jews* (New York: Alfred Knopf, 1968), 5th ed., p. 76.

23. James H. Breasted, *The Dawn of Conscience* (New York: Scribner's, 1968 [1933]), p. 384.

24. Breasted places great weight on the Wisdom of Amenemope (Amenempt), which probably dates from late in the second or early in the first millennium B.C., but the tract focuses primarily on the practical aspects of personal virtue. See E. A. Wallis Budge, *The Teaching of Amenemapt, Son of Kanekht* (London: Martin Hopkins, 1925), pp. 130–139. Crane Brinton's summary is to the point: "Even at the height of the [Egyptian] culture, however, we cannot possibly . . . outline an Egyptian equivalent of the Hebrew prophet, the Greek beautiful-and-good, the European knight of chivalry." In *A History of Western Morals* (New York: Harcourt, Brace, and World, 1959), p. 45.

25. Abraham J. Heschel, *The Prophets* (New York: Harper and Row, 1975 [1962]), vol. 2, pp. 254–262.

26. Emphasis added. The translation is that of the Hebrew Bible found in *The Holy Scriptures According to the Masoretic Text* (Philadelphia: Jewish Publication Society of America, 1955). The King James version is identical. A meaning that is more in keeping with the Hebrew mighty stream is winter-flowing, or a stream that never runs dry.

27. Heschel, *The Prophets*, vol. 1, p. 201.

28. Hebrew scholars leave little doubt that the words actually used for justice and righteousness (*mispat* and *sedakah*, respectively) bear separate meanings. See Johannes Lindblom, *Prophesy in Ancient Israel* (Philadelphia: Fortress Press, 1962), p. 312.

29. Related to, but more limited than, Micah's much-quoted statement is Justinian's comment: "The precepts of the law are to live honestly, to injure no one, and to give every man his due," found in *The Institutes* I, 1.3–4, Moyle translation (Oxford: Clarendon Press, 1967 [1883]), p. 3. Justinian's reference is plainly legal, but only faintly ethical. The fundamental distinction between the legal, on the one hand, and the ethical, on the other, was recently recognized by an artist as applying to his own field of endeavor. In John Updike's words: "The abiding mystery is not what art is for but what force it is that seizes the artist and makes him exceed the requirements of the market. This excess, strangely, is what we truly value." (Copyright John Updike, in *The New Yorker*, January 31, 1983, p. 123. Reprinted by permission.)

30. Johannes Lindblom, *Prophesy in Ancient Israel*, p. 352. See also A. B. Y. Scott, *The Relevance of the Prophets* (New York: Macmillan, 1944), p. 167.

31. Lindblom, *Prophesy in Ancient Israel*, pp. 333–335.

32. Immanuel Jakobovits, *Jewish Medical Ethics* (New York: Bloch, 1975 [1959]), pp. 211, 225–226.

33. Babylonian Talmud (London: Soncino Press, 1935), *Seder Nezekin*, *Baba Mezia* I, 30b (pp. 188–189).

34. *Baba Mezia*, 83a (p. 475).

35. Sussmann Munter, "Medicine in Ancient Israel," in Julius Preuss, *Biblisch-talmudische Medizin* (New York: Ktav, 1971 [1911]), p. xix.

36. R. H. Charles, ed., *The Apocrypha and Pseudepigrapha of the Old Testament in English* (Oxford: Clarendon Press, 1972 [1913]), vol. 1: *Apocrypha*. The passage quoted is on pages 448–449.

37. Jakobovits, *Jewish Medical Ethics*, p. 221.

38. Jakobovits, *Jewish Medical Ethics*, pp. 219–220. See also Julius Preuss, *Biblical and Talmudic Medicine*, trans. Fred Rosner (New York: Hebrew Publishing, 1983), pp. 22–31.

39. The Tosephta, *Baba Kama* 9:11 (Edition Zuckermandel [Hebrew text], Passewalk, 1881). The Tosephta (literally *addenda*) contains many regulations pertaining to physicians but is not available in English translation. Its relationship, to the Talmud itself and its authorship are in doubt. So also is its date, which is variously fixed from the third to the fifth centuries A.D.

40. Babylonian Talmud, *Seder Nezikin, Baba Kama*, chapter 1, 2a (p. 1). Chapter 8, 83b–93a (pp. 471–540) sets out five types of injury (depreciation, pain, healing, loss of time, and degradation) as well as tables of monetary compensation for specific injuries.

41. B. B. Liebermann, "Torts in Jewish Law," in *Studies in Jewish Jurisprudence* (New York: Herman Press, 1926), vol. 2, pp. 231–232.

42. Liebermann, "Torts in Jewish Law," p. 236.

43. *Maimonides' Code of Law and Ethics, Mishneh Torah* (New York: Hebrew Publishing Company, 1974 [1944]), p. 240. See also *The Code of Maimonides, Book Eleven: The Book of Torts* (New Haven: Yale University Press, 1954), treatise 5, chapter 13, p. 236. Maimonides' (born A.D. 1135, died 1204) *Mishneh Torah* (book XI) is especially important in present connections because it sets out Talmudic law on damages and compensation in accessible and readable form. Also relevant is *Code of Jewish Law, Kitzur, Shulhan Uruk* (New York: Hebrew Publishing Company, 1961), rev. ed., vol. 4, chap. 192, pp. 84–86, which deals with the sick, the physician, and remedies.

CHAPTER 2

1. Karl Jaspers, *The Origin and Goals of History* (New Haven: Yale University Press, 1953), pp. 1–2.

2. Cyrus H. Gordon, *The Common Background of Greek and Hebrew Civilization* (New York: W. W. Norton, 1965), pp. 279–300.

3. According to the Hebrew Bible and the Old Testament, Noah's three sons populated the earth after the flood (Genesis 9:18). Traditionally, it was Noah's third son Japheth and his grandson Javan whose progeny populated the regions around the Black and Caspian Seas and the Aegean islands. The name Javan came later to refer in Hebrew to Greeks or Greece. In Isaiah (66:19) there is reference in this sense to the escape of Babylonian exiles to "Tubal and Javan, to the isles afar off." In Joel (3:6) the prophet condemns the selling of Hebrews to the "sons of Javanim, that yet might move them far from their borders." In Ezekiel (27:13) Javan is mentioned as a merchant trading in slaves and brass objects. But there is no reference to cultural exchange at a higher level.

4. See generally T. B. L. Webster, *From Mycenae to Homer* (New York: W. W. Norton, 1964), especially chap. 8, pp. 208–258.

5. Denys L. Page, *History and the Homeric Iliad* (Berkeley: University of California Press, 1959), pp. 41–58 and 73–74.

6. Herodotus, *The History*, book 11, line 53 (LCL 117), p. 341.

7. W. F. Forrest, *The Emergence of Greek Democracy, 800–400 B.C.* (New York: World University Library, 1976 [1966]). See especially pp. 35–36.

8. M. I. Finley, *The Ancient Economy* (Berkeley: University of California Press, 1975), pp. 29–34.

9. W. K. C. Guthrie, *A History of Greek Philosophy* (Cambridge: Cambridge University Press, 1978 [1962]), vol. 1, pp. 7–8.

10. Plato, *Phaedo*, 95E45 108C (LCL 36), pp. 331–373.

11. Forrest, *Emergence of Greek Democracy*, pp. 45–66.

12. As recorded by Thucydides, *History of the Peloponnesian War* II, 34–46 (LCL 108), pp. 319–341. Thucydides may well have been in the audience.

13. There is fair consistency in Plato's opposition to Pericles' political views as stated in *Republic* VIII, 557D–558C (LCL 276), pp. 287–291, and *Gorgias*, 515D–518E (LCL 166), pp. 495–505. He sets out his ideas on justice and equality in laws 744B-C and 757A-E (LCL 187), p. 379 and 744B-C, pp. 413–415. Plato on slavery is best judged by comments in *Laws* VI, 776–778 (LCL 187), pp. 473–477. See also Glenn R. Morrow, "Plato and Greek Slavery," *Mind* 48:186–201 (1939); and Gregory Vlastos, "Does Slavery Exist in Plato's *Republic?*" *Classical Philosophy* 63:291–295 (1968). Aristotle's views on democracy and oligarchy are set out in *Politics* VI, 1318b (LCL 264), pp. 497–498. He also comes down solidly, as did Plato, in favor of a caste system (*Politics* VII, viii–ix; 1329a–b; pp. 575–583).

14. Werner Fite, *The Platonic Legend* (New York: Charles Scribner's Sons, 1934), pp. 128–152. R. H. S. Crossman expressed similar views in *Plato Today* (London: Allen and Unwin, 1937), pp. 129–133.

15. Karl R. Popper, *The Open Society and Its Enemies* (Princeton: Princeton University Press, 1966), vol. 1, *Plato*, 5th ed., p. vii. All of chapters 3, 6, and 10 are relevant. Popper compares the closed society to a ". . . tribe in being a semi-organic unit whose members are held together by semi-biologic ties—kinship, living together" (p. 173).

16. Ernest Barker, *Greek Political Theory: Plato and His Predecessors* (New York: Barnes and Noble, 1960 [1918]), 5th ed., pp. 28–31.

17. Diogenes Laertius, vol. 1 (LCL 184), p. 415. George Thomson quotes the same source in *Studies in Ancient Greek Society* (New York: Citadel Press, 1965 [1949]), pp. 33, 104–109.

18. M. S. Houdart, *Histoire de la médicine grècque depuis Esculape jusqu'à Hippocrate exclusivement* (Paris: J. B. Baillière, 1856). The author listed eighteen generations, beginning with Asklepius and continuing through Podaleiraus and ultimately through Hippocrates I, Heraclide, and Hippocrates the Great. Counting three generations to the century, and assuming that Hippocrates was born about 460 B.C., Asklepius would appear to have lived in the eleventh century B.C., and was thus pre-Homeric, whatever his actual genesis. See also Francis Adams *The Genuine Works of Hippocrates* (New York: William Wood, n.d. [1849]), p. 19.

19. Emma J. Edelstein and Ludwig Edelstein, *Asklepius: A Collection and Interpretation of the Testimonies* (Baltimore: Johns Hopkins University Press, 1945), 2 vols.

20. *Iliad* ii, 729 (LCL 170), p. 105. The same iv, 199 (LCL 170), p. 167. The same xi, 520 (LCL 170), p. 519. To the Greeks, Asklepius was noble and illustrious but not a god. The physician serving the Olympian Twelve

was Paiaon, a name vaguely associated with Apollo, who was second only to Zeus himself. See C. Kerenyi, *Asklepios: Archetypal Image of the Physician's Existence* (New York: Pantheon, 1959), pp. xvi–xviii and 80–81. Later authors, notably Lucian writing in the second century A.D., placed Asklepius among the Olympians. See *Dialogues of the Gods* 15 (13) (LCL 431), pp. 312–317. See also J. D. Rolleston, "Lucian and Medicine," *Proc. Roy. Soc. Med.* 8:49–84, at pp. 72–73.

21. Pausanias, *Description of Greece*, II (Corinth) 26.5–10 (LCL 93), pp. 387–391. Appollodorus, *The Library* III.x.3–4 (LCL 122), pp. 11–21. There is a Homeric hymn to Asklepius, possibly composed about 600 B.C. (LCL 57, p. 441). Pindar's account of the Asklepian legend leaves no doubt that Asklepius himself was mortal; see *Third Pythian Ode* (LCL 56), pp. 185–195. Guthrie in *The Greeks and Their Gods* (Boston: Beacon Press, 1950), pp. 242–253, says that Apollo was the healing *god*, but his quasi-mortal son Asklepius was the hero to whom the sick of ancient Europe turned for relief from infirmity.

22. Alison Burford, *The Greek Temple Builders at Epidaurus* (Toronto: University of Toronto Press, 1969), pp. 15–21.

23. C. Kerenyi, *Asklepios*, pp. 47–48.

24. Claudius Galen, *Opera Omnia*, ed. C. G. Kühn (Lipsiae: Car. Cnoblochii, 1821), book 2, *On Anatomical Procedures*, p. 281. Also in translation: trans. Charles Singer, Wellcome Historical Museum (London: Oxford University Press, 1956), pp. 31–32. Galen says that the art *(techne)* had once been customarily imparted to Asklepian kinsmen but came later to be no longer exclusive to the Asklepian family.

25. E. and L. Edelstein, *Asklepius*, p. 57. Galen also used Asklepian in a generic sense. See *Opera Omnia*, book X, p. 4; book XIII, p. 273; book XIV, p. 676.

26. E. T. Withington, "The Asclepiadae and the Priests of Asclepius," in *Studies in the History and Method of Science*, ed. Charles Singer (Oxford: Clarendon Press, 1921), vol. 2, pp. 192–205.

27. The story of the Alexandrian library and center of learning is to be found in Edward A. Parsons, *The Alexandrian Library: Glory of the Hellenic World* (New York: Elsevier, 1952). Its destruction is described by Alexandra Soterion in her "Book-burning," part I, *Book Arts* 2:26–34 (1977). The destruction of the library and center took place over many centuries, and the loss to civilization was so enormous that Christian, Jew, and Moslem, all of whom may have had a hand in it, still blame each other. See also Rudolph Pfeiffer, *History of Classical Scholarship* (Oxford: Clarendon Press, 1968), chapters 1–6, who describes the ". . . living chain of ancient personalities that had stretched from Philitas and Zenodotus to Aristarchus" (p. 233), covering approximately the span from 300 B.C. to 145 B.C.

28. These, in general, are the views of W. H. S. Jones in "Hippocrates

and the Corpus Hippocraticum," *Proc. British Acad.* 31:1–23 (1945), pp. 11–13. Edelstein's earlier article, "The Genuine Works of Hippocrates," *Bull. Hist. Med.* 7:236–248 (1939) leans heavily on the allegation that "Plato and Meno give enough details so as to make clear the outlines of Hippocratic medicine" (p. 143). Works that are at odds with those outlined, should, according to Edelstein, be excluded from the Corpus. This, to Jones, is easier said than done. The references to Plato with which both Jones and Edelstein are concerned are Protagoras, 311 B.C. (LCL 165), pp. 98–103, and Phaedo 270 c, D (LCL 36), pp. 548–549. Aristotle's comment is in *Politics* VII, 4, 3–5 (1326 a) (LCL 264), pp. 554–555. Menon is quoted from Anonymus Londinensis, a translation of which is included in the article by Jones cited above (pp. 4–5).

29. Hippocrates, *The Sacred Disease* (On Epilepsy I) 1–4 (LCL 148), p. 139; also John Chadwick and W. N. Mann, *The Medical Works of Hippocrates* (Oxford: Blackwell Scientific Publications, 1950), p. 179. See also Hippocrates, *Ancient Medicine*, I (LCL 147), pp. 13–15.

30. W. H. S. Jones, *Hippocrates, with an English translation* (Cambridge: Harvard University Press, 1922), general introduction. Hippocrates, (LCL 147), p. xxviii. Most of the works accepted as "Hippocratic" were identified by commentators writing before the second century A.D., and many were cited by Galen. See E. Littré, *Oeuvres complètes d'Hippocrate: Traduction nouvelle* (Paris: J. B. Baillière, 1839), vol. 1, ch. 5, pp. 80–132. See also Francis Adams, *Genuine Works of Hippocrates*, Preliminary Discourse, pp. 3–340. Adams took as criterion the acceptance of the treatise in question by at least one of the ancient authorities (p. 40). Erotian is the pre-Galenic source for commentators on Hippocratic treatises (see note 33 below).

31. Jones, *Hippocrates*, p. xxi.

32. Jones, *Hippocrates*, pp. xxvii and 296.

33. Erotiani Graeci, *Scriptoris Vetustissimi vocum, quae apud Hippocratem sunt Collectio* (Venetiis, apud Lucam Antonium, 1566), verso, p. 2. Erotian also lists 88 authors who wrote on themes relating to Hippocrates (leaf 4, unnumbered, after preface by Batholeomeu Eustachius).

34. Scribonius Largus, *Compositiones*, ed. G. Helmreich (Leipzig: B. G. Teubner, 1877), pp. 2–4.

35. W. H. S. Jones, *The Doctor's Oath* (Cambridge: Cambridge University Press, 1924), p. 44. See also W. H. S. Jones, *Hippocrates*, p. xlii.

36. Francis Adams, *Genuine Works of Hippocrates*, p. 24. Adams wrote: "But, upon the whole, all must allow that Galen is our best guide on the subject of our present inquiry."

37. W. H. S. Jones, *Hippocrates*, pp. lxiii–lxiv.

38. E. Littré, *Oeuvres complètes d'Hippocrate*, vol. 4, pp. 610–633.

39. Francis Adams, *Genuine Works of Hippocrates*, p. 38.

40. Karl Deichgräber, "Die ärztliche Standesethik des hippokratischen

Eides," *Quellen und Studien zur Geschichte der Naturwissenschaften und der Medizin* 3:29–49 (1932).

41. W. H. S. Jones, *Hippocrates*, pp. 40–41.

42. Savas Nittis, "The Authorship and Probable Date of the Hippocratic Oath," *Bull. Hist. Med.* 8:1012–1021 (July 1940).

43. Charles Victor Daremberg, *Hippocrate* (Paris: Chez Lefévre, 1843), p. 1.

44. W. H. S. Jones, "Hippocrates and the Corpus Hippocraticum," p. 44.

45. Robert Fuchs, "Geschichte der Heilkunde bei den Griechen," in *Handbuch der Geschichte der Medizin*, ed. Th. Puschmann (Jena: Gustav Fischer, 1901), p. 224.

46. Thomson, *Studies in Ancient Greek Society*, p. 333, note 6.

47. Ludwig Edelstein, "The Hippocratic Oath: Text, Translation, and Interpretation," in *Ancient Medicine: Selected Papers of Ludwig Edelstein* (Baltimore: Johns Hopkins University Press, 1967), pp. 3–63. Originally published as Supplement No. 1 to the *Bull. Hist. Med.* (1943). The Oath is at p. 6.

48. C. J. DeVogel, *Pythagoras and Early Pythagoranism* (Assem: Van Goreum, 1966), pp. 232–244.

49. DeVogel, *Pythagoras and Early Pythagoranism*, pp. 176–180. See also Diodorus Siculus, X.9, 1–4 (LCL 375), pp. 66–67.

50. Edelstein, "The Hippocratic Oath," p. 44.

51. Diodorus Siculus, X.9, 1 (LCL 375), p. 67.

52. Edelstein, "The Hippocratic Oath," pp. 50–51. But he seems somewhat ambivalent about assigning *all* features of the Oath's covenant to Pythagorean custom and teaching. With regard to the covenant he says that its various demands may ". . . be explained only in connection with Pythagorean views and customs, *or at least they are compatible with them*" (p. 44; emphasis added).

53. Edelstein, "The Hippocratic Oath," pp. 53–54.

54. Edelstein, "The Hippocratic Oath," p. 63.

55. Alfred Zimmern, *The Greek Commonwealth* (New York: Modern Library, n.d.), 5th ed., p. 262.

56. W. F. J. Knight, *Many-Minded Homer* (New York: Barnes and Noble, 1968), pp. 64–65. See also Gustave Glotz, *Ancient Greece at Work* (New York: W. W. Norton, 1967 [1920]. "In the liberal careers . . . the schools of medicine and music were family groups." So also with sculpture, painting, architecture, and other vocations (pp. 21, 266, 361).

57. Ludwig Edelstein, "The Hippocratic Physician," in *Ancient Medicine: Selected Papers by Ludwig Edelstein* (Baltimore: Johns Hopkins University Press, 1967 [1931]), pp. 87–110.

58. Edelstein, "The Hippocratic Physician," p. 88n.

59. *The Law* (date uncertain), *Precepts* (100 B.C.–A.D. 100), *On the Physician* (350–300 B.C.) and *Decorum* (300 B.C. or later). The dates are those given by Jones (LCL 147–150).

60. *Odyssey* XXII.1–501; XXIV.465–476 (LCL 105), pp. 337–373 and 437–439.

61. *Iliad* XVII.495–508 (LCL 171), pp. 325–327. See also the Fitzgerald translation (New York: Anchor, 1975), p. 451.

62. Robert J. Bonner and Gertrude Smith, *The Administration of Justice from Homer to Aristotle* (Chicago: University of Chicago Press, 1930), vol. 1, pp. 31–41. See also Douglas MacDowell's volume, *The Law in Classical Athens* (London: Thames and Hudson, 1978), pp. 18–21 and 32–33. Hildebrecht Hommel places the date of the shield scene in Homer's day or later. See "Die Gerichtsszene auf dem Schild des Achillaus," in *Politeia und Res Publica*, ed. Peter Steinmetz (Wiesbaden: Frank Steiner, 1969), pp. 11–38. The best account in English is Hans Wolff, "The Origin of Judicial Litigation Among the Greeks," *Traditio* 4:31–87 (1946).

63. Strabo, *The Geography*, VI.L.i (LCL 182), pp. 31–33. At the end of the section, Strabo quotes Plato rather inaccurately as saying that ". . . where there are many laws there are also many lawsuits . . . just as where there are many physicians there are also likely to be many diseases." Plato has something of the sort to say, in many more words, in *The Republic* 405A–405E (LCL 237), pp. 256–273.

64. *Plutarch's Lives*, Solon XVII (LCL 46), pp. 449–451.

65. Russell Meiggs and David Lewis, *A Selection of Greek Historical Inscriptions to the End of the Fifth Century B.C.* (Oxford: Clarendon Press, 1969), pp. 264–265.

66. Aristotle, *The Athenian Constitution*, VII.1 (LCL 285), p. 25.

67. MacDowell, *Law in Classical Athens*, pp. 109–122.

68. Ronald F. Willetts, *The Law Code of Gortyn* (Berlin: Walter de Gruyter, 1967). The volume includes a legible photocopy of the original law and a copy of a rubbing originally prepared by Comparetti.

69. Willetts, *Law Code of Gortyn*, p. 40.

70. *Odyssey*, VIII.266–349 (LCL 104), pp. 277–283.

71. Antiphon, *Third Tetralogy*, III.4–6 (LCL 308), p. 135.

72. Darrell Amundsen, "The Liability of the Physician and Classical Greek Theory and Practice," *J. Hist. Med. and Allied. Sci.* 32:171–203 (1977).

73. Plato, *The Laws*, IX.865, B (LCL 192), p. 239. The exact quote (Bury translation) is: ". . . if the patient dies against the will of his doctor, the doctor shall be accounted legally pure."

74. Plato, *The Laws*, IV.720, B.E. (LCL 187), pp. 309–311.

75. Aristotle, *The Politics*, III.xi.5 (LCL 264), p. 265.

76. Aristotle, *The Politics*, III.vi.8 (LCL 264), pp. 225–227.

77. J. C. Stobart, *The Glory that Was Greece*, edited and revised by R. J. Hopper (London: Sedgwick and Jackson, 1976 [1911]), 4th ed., p. vi.

CHAPTER 3

1. Horace cites them reverently in his epistle to Lollius Maximus, found in *Epistles* II (LCL 194), pp. 260–267; so also did many others, including Virgil, Lucretius, Cicero, Livy, and Juvenal.

2. Horace, *Epistles* II, 11.156–157 (LCL 194), pp. 408–409.

3. Livy says that a deputation of three patricians was sent in 456 B.C. to Athens "to copy the famous laws of Solon and to acquaint themselves with the institutions, customs, and laws of the other Greek states;" see *The Early History of Rome* III.31.8 (LCL 133), p. 107. Dionysius of Halicarnassus mentions "Greek laws brought back by the ambassadors," presumably the three named by Livy; see *Roman Antiquities* X.55.5 (LCL 378), p. 353.

4. A. C. Johnson, P. R. Coleman-Norton, and F. C. Bourne, *Ancient Roman Statutes* (Austin: University of Texas Press, 1961), pp. 9–18. See also W. H. Warmington, *Remains of Old Latin III: Laws of the XII Tables* (LCL 329), pp. xxvi–xxxiii and 424–510.

5. Ovid, *The Metamorphoses* xv.625–744 (LCL 43), pp. 409–417. Livy also tells of the arrival of Asklepius at Rome in *Annals of Rome* X.47.6–7, and *Libri* XI, *Periocha* (LCL 191), pp. 542–543 and 546–547.

6. Pliny the Elder, *Natural History* 29.I.VII (LCL 418), pp. 182–201.

7. Pliny, *Natural History*, pp. 187–191. Many Greek physicians came as slaves and some were later freed. Some took Latin names. One such was Vettus Valens, who was among the many who dallied with Messalina, wife of the Emperor Claudius.

8. F. H. Lawson, *Negligence in the Civil Law* (Oxford: Clarendon Press, 1950), p. 4.

9. Justinian, Digest IX.2.7. Found in Justinian, *The Digest of Roman Law: Theft, Rapine, Damage and Insult*, trans. C. F. Kolbert (Hardmondsworth: Penguin Books, 1979), p. 73. The complete Corpus Juris of Justinian was inadequately translated by S. P. Scott in *The Civil Law* (Cincinnati: Central Trust Company, 1932, 17 vols.; reprint ed. New York: AMS Press, 1932, 17 vols. compressed into 7).

10. Justinian, *Digest* IX.2.52, p. 75.

11. Justinian, *Digest* IX.2.9, p. 75. But in Roman Law, negligence had no precisely defined meaning comparable to the definition that has evolved in Anglo-American common law.

12. Lawson, *Negligence in the Civil Law*, pp. 21–27. See also Alan Watson, *The Law of Obligation in the Later Roman Republic* (Oxford: Clarendon Press, 1965), pp. 234–235. Also Rudolph Sohn, *The Institutes: History and*

System of Roman Law (1940, 3rd ed; New York: Rothman Reprints, 1970), pp. 417–425.

13. Usually attributed to Hugo Grotius, *De jure ac pacis libri tres*, trans. Francis W. Kelley (Oxford: Clarendon Press, 1925), vol. 2, pp. 430–437. Grotius wrote in the seventeenth century (1625) but, as will be shown, English common law developed special considerations in the fourteenth century to apply to doctors who were negligent.

14. Justinian, *Digest* IX.2.9, p. 75.

15. *Delictum* in Latin meant (literally) fault or crime. The Roman law of delicts provided legal remedies for damage to person or property, whether the wrongdoer was doctor or layman. Negligence is implied in Book IX of the *Digest* of Justinian in many places, the Latin word usually being *culpa* (fault, or blame). For example, in the *Digest* IX.2.31, p. 91: ". . . there is fault when what could have been foreseen by a diligent man was not foreseen." The phrase diligent man is the ancestor of the common law's reasonable or prudent man. See apocryphal *Fardell v. Potts* in A. P. Herbert, *Uncommon Law* (London: Eyre Methuen, 1974), pp. 1–6.

16. Joseph Vogt, *Ancient Slavery and the Ideal of Man* (Oxford: Basil, Blackwell, 1974), pp. 114–118.

17. Caesar's gesture in favor of physicians (46 B.C.) is mentioned by Suetonius in *Lives of the Caesars* I.42.1 (LCL 31), p. 59. Vespasian exempted physicians from taxation and lawsuits (Johnson, *Ancient Roman Statutes*, statute 185, p. 151). Vibius, prefect of Egypt, exempted physicians (and others) from public duties in A.D. 103 (Johnson, *Ancient Roman Statutes*, statute 207, p. 166), and Julian (A.D. 362) reaffirmed edicts of earlier emperors favoring physicians (Johnson, *Ancient Roman Statutes*, statute 312, p. 243). The Theodosian Code contains a summary of actions in favor of physicians in general, and of the "chief physicians of the sacred imperial palace," in particular, by various emperors, including Constantine, Valentinian, and Theodosius. See *Theodosian Code* XIII.3.1–19 (reprint ed. New York: Greenwood Press, 1969), pp. 385–390. The dates range from A.D. 320 to A.D. 428.

18. John Scarborough, *Roman Medicine* (London: Thames and Hudson, 1969), pp. 109–121.

19. A. J. Brock, *Galen on the Natural Faculties*, LCL 71, p. ix.

20. H. I. Marrou, *A History of Education in Antiquity* (London: Sheed and Ward, 1956), pp. 288–289.

21. Quintillian, *Institutio oratoria* XII, 1.24–26 and XII 3.1–12 (LCL 127), pp. 375 and 401–407.

22. Vitruvius, *The Ten Books on Architecture* (New York: Dover, 1960), book I, chapter 1, pp. 5–13. Also LCL 251, I.c.i., pp. 7–25. Italics added.

23. Galen, *On the Natural Faculties*, LCL 179, pp. 279–280.

24. Scarborough, *Roman Medicine*, pp. 122–123. See also Marrou, *History of Education in Antiquity*, pp. 192–193.

25. Ludwig Edelstein, "The Professional Ethics of the Greek Physician," *Bull. Hist. Med.* 30:391–419 (1956). See also Karl Deichgräber, "Professio Medici: Zum Vorwort des Scribonius Largus," *Abhandl. der geistes und sozialwissensch. Klasse* 9:855–879 (1950).

26. Cicero usually refers to doctors and to medicine to make an unrelated point by analogy. In Book I, he lumps physicians, generals, and orators together, adding that members of all three callings have a duty to discharge (I.viii). Also in Book I, he speaks of medicine, architecture, and teaching as callings that require a high degree of intelligence and that confer ". . . no small benefit on society" (I.xlii; LCL 30, pp. 63 and 155).

27. *De Officiis* III.xv, 61–64. The entire dialogue is III.xi–xviii (LCL 30, pp. 319–347).

28. Plato, in this connection, specified both rulers and physicians. The former should should not "consider and enjoin his own advantage but that of the one whom he rules and for whom he exercises his craft." As for the latter, Plato says that no physician ". . . in so far as he is a physician seek[s] or enjoin[s] the advantage of the physician but that of the patient." See *The Republic*, I.342 D–E (LCL 237), pp. 62–63. Plato, expressing an ideal rather than actual conditions, was ahead of his time.

29. As emphasized by Edelstein in "Professional Ethics of the Greek Physician," pp. 340–344. See also, e.g., Cicero's *De Finibus* III.xi.36 (LCL 40), p. 255.

30. Scribonius Largus, *Compositiones*, ed. G. Helmreich (Leipzig: B. G. Teubner, 1887). The introduction (in Latin) is appended to Deichgräber's article "Professio Medici," pp. 875–879. There is no English rendering, although a translation of the introduction is currently in preparation by Jeffrey S. Hamilton in *Scribonius Largus and Professio* (forthcoming).

31. Scribonius, *Compositiones*, p. 2, line 27.

32. Scribonius, *Compositiones*, p. 2, lines 17–18. The meaning of humanities, according to Edelstein ("Professional Ethics of the Greek Physician," p. 338 n. 33) is that given by Gellius ". . . the meaning which it [humanitas] is commonly thought to have . . . [is] what the Greeks call φιλανθρωπία, signifying a kind of friendly spirit and good-feeling toward all men without distinction. . . ." The purists give humanitas a more restricted meaning: something to do with "education and training in the liberal arts." See *Attic Nights of Aulus Gellius* XIII. 17 (LCL 200), p. 457.

33. Scribonius, *Compositiones*, p. 4, lines 18–23.

34. Scribonius, *Compositiones*, p. 5, lines 3–5.

35. Scribonius, *Compositiones*, p. 3, lines 6–8. See also Edelstein, "Professional Ethics of the Greek Physician," p. 338.

36. Edelstein, "Professional Ethic of the Greek Physician," p. 339. This, approximately, is what Edelstein means by medical humanism. "That such an ideal of medical humanism is foreign to the spirit of Hippocratic ethics, Scribonius admits himself" (pp. 339–340).

37. Seneca, *De Beneficiis* VI, xv. 2–5 (LCL 310), pp. 393–397.

38. James H. Oliver, "An Ancient Poem on the Duties of a Physician," *Bull. Hist. Med.* 7:315–323 (1939).

39. J. P. Waltzing, *Étude historique sur les corporations professionnelles chez les Romains* (1889; reprint ed. New York: Hildesheim, 1970), vol. 1, pp. 32–56; vol. 2, p. 132; vol. 4, p. 29 (item 29). See also T. R. S. Broughton, "Roman Asia," in *An Economic Survey of Ancient Rome* (New York: Farrar, Straus, and Giroux, 1975), vol. 4, pp. 841–845 and 851–853.

40. Johnson, *Ancient Roman Statutes*, statute 185, p. 151. The precedent for such an action was in the Twelve Tables, which authorized the organization of guilds that could make any rules they wished so long as they were not in conflict with public law. See Johnson, *Ancient Roman Statutes*, document 8, VIII.27, p. 12.

41. M. Rostovtzeff, *The Social and Economic History of the Roman Empire*, 2nd ed. (Oxford: Clarendon Press, 1957), vol. 1, pp. 19–191.

42. Begun, on Justinian's order, by Tribonius and sixteen assistants in late A.D. 530. See H. F. Jolowicz and Berry Nicholas, *Historical Introduction to the Study of Roman Law*, 3rd ed. (Cambridge: Cambridge University Press, 1972), pp. 479–491.

43. Edward Gibbon, *Decline and Fall of the Roman Empire* (New York: Modern Library, n.d.), vol. 2, pp. 1441–1450.

44. J. B. Bury, *The Invasion of Europe by the Barbarians* (New York: W. W. Norton, 1967 [1928]).

45. Richard Mansfield Haywood, *The Myth of Rome's Fall* (New York: Thomas Y. Crowell, 1962 [1958]), pp. 155–164.

46. Haywood, *Myth of Rome's Fall*, p. 154.

47. Thanks in no small measure to Rome's aristocracy. See M. L. W. Laistner, *Christianity and Pagan Culture in the Later Roman Empire* (Ithaca: Cornell University Press, 1951), p. 6.

48. Haywood, *Myth of Rome's Fall*, p. 168.

49. Frederick Pollock and Frederick Wilhelm Maitland, *The History of English Law Before the Time of Edward I* (Cambridge: University Press, 1968 [1895], vol. 1, p. 5. Alaric's Breviary contains a section on obligation *ex delicto* that is obviously Roman. See Conrat-Cohn, Brevarium Alaricianum: *Römisches Recht im Fränkeschen Reich* (Leipzig: J. C. Hinrich, 1903), III.2.3. a–c. See also Ernst Levy, "Reflections on the First Reception of Roman Law in Germanic States," *Amer. Hist. Rev.* 48:26–29 (1943).

50. P. D. King, *Law and Society in the Visigothic Kingdom* (Cambridge: Cambridge University Press, 1972), pp. 1–22.

51. Carolus Zeumer, *Leges Visgothorum* (Hanover and Leipzig: Bibl. Hahn., 1902), tomus 1, *Leges Nationum Germanicarum*, pp. 400–403 (Latin only). Also Fred Walter, *Corpus juris Germanici antiqui: Legis Wisigothorum* Lib. XI, Tit. 1 (Berolini: G. Reimeri, 1824), vol. 1, pp. 626–627 (Latin only); Eugen Wohlhaupter, *Gesetze der Westgoten* (Berlin: Hermann Bohlhaus, 1936), X.1, 1–14, pp. 290–293. See also Darrell Amundsen, "Visigothic Medical Legislation," *Bull. Hist. Med.* 45:553–569 (Nov.–Dec. 1971).

52. *Lex Visigothorum* XI.I.8.

53. *Digest of Justinian* (25.4.1.1; Scott, AMS reprint, vol. 3; vol. 6 of original edition; p. 44) says that ". . . the child is part of the woman or of her entrails before it is born." Nor can the unborn child of a slave woman itself be considered a slave (35.2.9.1; AMS reprint, vol. 4; vol. 6 of original edition; p. 7). But a woman could not produce an abortion on herself without her husband's concurrence (47.11.4; AMS reprint, vol. 5; vol. 10 of original edition; p. 328).

54. Katherine Fischer Drew, *The Burgundian Code* (Philadelphia: University of Pennsylvania Press, 1949), pp. 20–21.

55. Katherine Fischer Drew, *The Lombard Laws* (Philadelphia: University of Pennsylvania Press, 1973).

56. Tacitus, *Germania* 11–12 (LCL 35), pp. 147–151. See also P. V. Glob, *The Bog People: Iron-Age Man Preserved* (London: Faber and Faber, 1977 [1969]), pp. 90, 143, 153.

57. Tacitus, *Germania* 7 (LCL 35), p. 143.

58. Caesar, *The Gallic War* IV, 1–3 and VI, 21–24 (LCL 72), pp. 181–185 and 344–350.

CHAPTER 4

1. Tacitus, *Agricola* 24.3 (LCL 35), p. 71. Tacitus quoted Agricola, his father-in-law, as saying ". . . that with one legion and a fair contingent of irregulars Ireland could be overpowered and held. . . ." Agricola was Roman governor of Britain A.D. 78–87.

2. For example: Hadrian's rescript to Pompeius Falco when the latter (probably) was governor of Britain in *Digest of Justinian* 28.3.7 (AMS reprint, vol. 3), p. 201. Also Severus' rescript to Virius Lupus, Governor of Britain in *Digest of Justinian* 28.6.2.4 (AMS reprint, vol. 3), p. 240. A Roman centurion serving in Scotland (Coccius Firmus) was awarded the price of the ransom of a slave from the State Treasury in *Digest of Justinian* 49.15.6 (AMS reprint, vol. 5), p. 117, and a rescript of Constantine I gave instructions to one Pecatianus, a top official serving in Britain, concerning certain revenues due the state. See *Theodosian Code* 11.7.2, trans. Clyde Pharr (Princeton University Press, 1952; reprint ed. New York: Greenwood Press,

1969), p. 299. See also Eric Birley, *Roman Britain and the Roman Army* (Kendal: Titus Wilson and Son, 1953), chapt. 5, pp. 48–57.

3. Henry Marsh, *The Origins of the English People* (Newton Abbot: David and Charles, 1969), pp. 11–13. Also Bede, *A History of the English Church and People* (Harmondsworth: Penguin Books, 1975 [1955]), chapt. 15, pp. 55–57.

4. Translations of Anglo-Saxon law promulgated by Aethelbert, Ine, and Alfred (and others) are in F. L. Attenborough, *The Laws of the Earliest English Kings* (Cambridge: Cambridge University Press, 1922). Canute's law is in A. J. Robertson, *The Laws of the Kings of England from Edmund to Henry I* (Cambridge: Cambridge University Press, 1925).

5. Attenborough, *Laws of the Earliest English Kings*, pp. 87–93. Similar provisions were included in the Alamannic Laws (LVII, 1–69) of the eighth century A.D. See Theodore J. Rivers, *Laws of the Alamans and Bavarians* (Philadelphia: University of Pennsylvania Press, 1977), pp. 85–90.

6. Attenborough, *Laws of the Earliest English Kings*, p. 13.

7. Frederick Pollock and Frederic William Maitland, *The History of English Law*, 2nd ed. (Cambridge: Cambridge University Press, 1968 [1898]), vol. 1, p. 88.

8. Maitland (among others) conveys this impression in his *Constitutional History of England* (Cambridge: Cambridge University Press, 1913), pp. 7–9. See also William Stubbs, *On the English Constitution* (New York: Thomas Y. Crowell, 1966), pp. 19–51. G. O. Sayles, in his *The Medieval Foundation of England* (New York: A. S. Barnes, 1961 [1948]), attempts with some success to overcome his English bias in the matter (pp. 212–238).

9. R. C. Van Caenegem, *The Birth of English Common Law* (Cambridge: Cambridge University Press, 1973), pp. 11–12.

10. The last version, *Leges Henrici Primi*, trans. L. J. Downer (Oxford: Clarendon Press, 1972) was a modification of Canute's laws, dating from the early twelfth century. *Leges Henrici* included detailed tables of compensation not unlike those in Alfred's laws (Chapt. 93, pp. 293–301).

11. The importance and uniqueness of the Year Books as the early record of the common law is dealt with by Holdsworth in *History of English Law* (London: Methuen, 1971 [1903]), vol. 2, pp. 525–556.

12. Holdsworth, *History of English Law*, vol. 2, pp. 232–290. See especially pp. 267–280.

13. Bracton, *On the Laws and Customs of England*, trans. Samuel E. Thorne (Cambridge: Harvard University Press, 1968), vol. 2, pp. 289–290.

14. Bracton, *Laws and Customs of England*, vol. 2, p. 341.

15. *Digest of Justinian* (Kolbert) IX. 2.31 (Harmondsworth: Penguin Books, 1979), p. 91.

16. Bracton, *Laws and Customs of England*, vol. 2, p. 296.

17. Dramatized with some bias toward the church in T. S. Eliot's *Murder in the Cathedral*.

18. It still stands, the most impressive physical memorial to Anglo-American legal and political systems, nearly nine centuries after William II (Rufus) held court there in 1099. It was his most noteworthy achievement. In our own time it is somewhat dwarfed by the Gothic gingerbread of Barry's nineteenth-century Houses of Parliament. See generally Ivy M. Cooper, "Westminster Hall," *J. British Archaeol. Assoc.* 1 (series 3):168–228 (1937). Also *Roy. Comm. on Historical Monuments England: Vol. 2, West London* (H.M. Stationer's Office, 1925), pp. 121–123. Also *Peterborough Chronicle*, trans. Harry A. Rositzke (New York: Columbia University Press, 1951), pp. 122–135.

19. The writ of trepass at first covered both civil wrongs, for which the injured party sought compensation, and crimes which were prosecuted by the state. Trespass later came to refer entirely to civil wrongs and not to criminal matters. See S. F. C. Milsom, *Historical Foundations of the Common Law* (London: Butterworth's, 1969), pp. 244–245.

20. Milsom, *Historical Foundations of the Common Law*, pp. 261–265. The distinction between trespass and trespass on the case rested on fictions and technicalities that are not presently germane. But they survived long enough to be included in the law of some American states and, although mostly abandoned in Britain by the nineteenth century, they still surface occasionally in English court proceedings.

21. "Misfeasance by Surgeons," in A. K. R. Kiralfy, *A Source Book of English Law* (London: Sweet and Maxwell, 1957), p. 184.

22. *John the Warner v. Thomas the Leech.* In Kiralfy, *Source Book of English Law*, pp. 184–185.

23. Edward III pardoned both wrongdoers. The cases are cited by Madeleine Pelner Cosman, "Medieval Medical Malpractice: The Dicta and the Dockets," *Bull. New York Acad. Med.* 49 (Ser.2):22–47 (1973). The mayor and aldermen of London appointed competent surgeons and apothecaries to judge actions brought against members of their profession by patients who claimed to have suffered injury at their hands. A London ordinance of 1356 laid down standards for judging negligent or incompetent horse doctors. See H. T. Riley, *Memorials of London and London Life: 1276–1419* (London: Longmans, Green, n.d.), pp. 67, 273, 292–293, 337, 393–394, 464, 519–520, 606–609, and 651.

24. *Year Book 48, Edward 3, Hilary Term*, f.6, pl. 11. Included, along with corresponding plea roll, in Kiralfy's *A Source Book of English Law*, p. 185. Also in C. H. S. Fifoot, *History and Sources of the Common Law: Tort and Contracts* (London: Stevens and Sons, 1949), p. 82.

25. Italics added.

26. R. B. Dobson, *The Peasants' Revolt of 1381* (London: Macmillan, 1970), p. 160. Also *Anonimale Chronicle 1333 to 1381*, ed. V. H. Galbraith (Manchester: University Press, 1927), pp. 193–203. England's massive difficulties began in mid-century with a devastating visitation of bubonic plague. Laborers were suddenly in short supply and Parliament, as a consequence, passed an ill-considered statute requiring every able-bodied laborer under fifty to work or go to jail. Wages were set at the pre-plague level and workers were required to serve out agreed-upon indentures. See *Statues at Large 23, Edward III*, 1349, vol. 2, pp. 26–30. Trouble was not long in coming.

27. *Waldon v. Mareschal, Year Book 43, Edward III*, pl. 38, f.33, 1370. *The Farrier's Case, Year Book 46, Edward III*, pl. 19, f.19, 1373. Both are in Fifoot, *History and Sources of the Common Law*, pp. 81–82.

28. Hubert Smith, "Legal Responsibility for Medical Malpractice II: Malpractice: Something of the Anatomy of the Law," *J. Amer. Med. Assoc.* 116:2149–2159 (10 May 1941). Actually, Smith went no further back than Fitzherbert's *Natura Brevia* of 1534. But Fitzherbert cites *The Surgeon's Case (Stratton v. Swanlond)* and other *Year Book* cases. See *Natura Brevia*, 9th ed. (London: Strahan and Woodfall, 1794), vol. 1, 94D. From Fitzherbert, the lineage runs via eighteenth-and nineteenth-century English cases to *Leighton v. Sargent* (7 New Hampshire Rep. [Foster], 460 [1855]) and *McCandless v. McWha* (22 Penn Rep., 261 [1855]), which link the English common law of malpractice to the American.

29. Francis Bacon, *Works* (London: J. Crowder and E. Hemsted, 1803), vol. 4, p. 33 (Regula VII).

30. As set out by the Lord Chief Justice in *Slater v. Baker and Stapleton*, 1767 (95 English Rep., K. B. Div. 860).

31. Bede, *A History of the English Church and People* (Harmondsworth: Penguin Books, 1975 [1955]), p. 240. Payne covers Bede's writing and the centuries between Bede and the conquest in *English Medicine in Anglo-Saxon Times* (Oxford: Clarendon Press, 1904). Anglo-Saxon therapeutics and superstitions were only gradually replaced after the Conquest by those transmitted by Galen and Hippocrates. See Stanley Rubin, *Medieval English Medicine* (London: David and Charles, 1974), pp. 189–192. After the Council of Tours (1163), the clergy was forbidden to study or practice medicine, a proscription that was reiterated by Innocent III in 1215. After that date the clergy seems to have tended more and more to matters spiritual. As for the healers, a sort of stratification was under way, with the physicians on top, surgeons in the middle, and apothecaries (empirics) below; see Rubin, pp. 194–195.

32. Edward J. Kealey, *Medieval Medicus: A Social History of Anglo-Norman Medicine* (Baltimore: Johns Hopkins University Press, 1981), pp. 31–33.

Kealey includes, in an appendix, a detailed directory of ninety Anglo-Norman physicians who practiced in the first half of the twelfth century.

33. C. J. S. Thompson, *The Mystery and Art of the Apothecary* (London: Bodley Head, 1929), pp. 85–86.

34. Thompson, *Mystery and Art of the Apothecary*, p. 88.

35. Thompson, *Mystery and Art of the Apothecary*, pp. 179–180.

36. Sylvia L. Thrupp. *The Merchant Class of Medieval London* (Ann Arbor: University of Michigan Press, 1977 [1962]), pp. 14–15.

37. Charles E. Mallett, *A History of the University of Oxford* (London: Methuen, 1924), vol. 1, pp. 416–417. See also C. D. O'Malley, *English Medical Humanists; Thomas Linacre and John Caius* (Lawrence: Univeristy of Kansas Press, 1965).

38. George Clark, *A Hisotry of the Royal College of Physicians* (Oxford: Clarendon Press, 1964), vol. 1, pp. 42–45.

39. *Statutes at Large*, 3 Henry VIII, C. 11, vol. 3.

40. Edward Meryon, *The History of Medicine* (London: Longman, Green, Longman, and Roberts, 1861), vol. 1, p. 436, footnote.

41. A. P. Cawadias, "The Royal College of Physicians of London on the Occasion of Its Recent Bombing," *Proc. Roy. Soc.* 34:53–64 (October 1941).

42. Clark, *History of the Royal College of Physicians*, vol. 1, p. 63.

43. William Munk, *Roll of the Royal College of Physicians of London*, 2nd ed. (London: The College, 1878), vol. 1, pp. 2–6.

44. *Statutes at Large, 14 and 15 Henry VIII*, C.5, vol. iv, pp. 155–157.

45. *Statutes at Large, 1 Mary*, Sec. Sess., C.9, 1553, vol. 6, pp. 15–16.

46. "Nova et Ventura: Some Figures in Medical History: John Caius," *British Med. J.* 2:83–86 (12 July 1913). A more extensive biography of Caius, by Venn, is included in *The Works of John Caius* (Cambridge: Cambridge University Press, 1912), pp. 1–54. Other biographical sketches are Thomas Pettigrew, *Medical Portrait Gallery: Biographical Memoirs of Physicians and Surgeons* (London: Fisher, 1842), vol. 1, p. 8, and G. G. Bettany, *Eminent Doctors: Their Lives and Their Work* (London: John Hogg, n.d.), vol. 1, pp. 13–23.

47. W. Osler, "Men and Books: The Works of John Caius," *Canad. Med. Asso. J.* 2:1034–1036 (November 1912).

48. "Nova et Ventura," p. 83.

49. Ioannis Caii, *Britanni De Libris Suis* (London: William Seversum, 1570), Liber Unus, 10a (last 4 lines), p. 81. Included in facsimile in *Works of John Caius*.

50. Clark, *History of the Royal College of Physicians*, vol. 1, pp. 93–94.

51. Clark, *History of the Royal College of Physicians*, vol. 1, pp. 109–110. For example, John Geynes, an Oxford man, was threatened with impris-

onment and forced to recant publicly because he declined to worship at the Galenic shrine.

52. Clark, *History of the Royal College of Physicians*, vol. 1, pp. 111–121. Also Charles Goodall, *The Royal College of Physicians of London* (London: M. Fletcher for Walter Kettilly, 1654). Goodall summarizes the proceedings against irregulars and empirics from the reign of Henry VIII to that of Charles I (pp. 305–472). Also included are the Charter of 1518 and Acts of Parliament relating to the College of Physicians.

53. Clark, *History of the Royal College of Physicians*, vol. 1, p. 95.

54. Clark, *History of the Royal College of Physicians*, vol. 1, p. 383. Italics added. See also pp. 180–181.

55. All of these versions are to be found in Clark, *History of the Royal College of Physicians:* the 1553 version is in vol. 1, pp. 376–392; the 1647 version is in vol. 1, pp. 393–417; the 1834 version is in vol. 2, pp. 744–767. All are in Latin.

56. *The Statutes of the College of Physicians, London* (London: Ship in St. Paul's Courtyard, 1698).

57. *Collegii Regalis Medicorum Londinensiu: Statuta Moralia* (London, 1722).

58. Royal College of Physicians of London, *Charter, By-Laws, and Regulations* (London, The College), 1882.

59. Royal College, *Charter, By-Laws, and Regulations*, by-laws 144 and 150.

60. Clark, *History of the Royal College of Physicians*, vol. 1, p. 32.

61. Sanford V. Larkey, "The Hippocratic Oath in Elizabethan England," in *Legacies in Ethics and Medicine*, ed. Chester R. Burns (New York: Science History Publications, 1977), pp. 218–236.

62. Clark, *History of the Royal College of Physicians*, vol. 1, p. 33.

63. London's population was relatively stable at about 50,000 from the twelfth to the early sixteenth centuries. Thereafter it rose slowly until the mid-eighteenth century, after which it began to rise more or less exponentially.

64. Clark, *History of the Royal College of Physicians*, vol. 2, pp. 736–739; vol. 3, pp. 1131–1133.

65. 8 *Coke Rep.*, 114 (1609) (London: E. & R. Nutt, and R. Gosling, 1727). 2 *Brownlow*, 255 (1609). Also 123 *English Rep.*, 928 (1609). See also S. E. Thorne, "Dr. Bonham's Case," 54 *Law Quart. Rev.* 543–522 (1938); J. W. Gough, *Fundamental Law in English Constitutional History* (Oxford: Clarendon Press, 1955), pp. 30–47; E. T. F. Plucknett, "Bonham's Case and Judicial Review," 40 *Harvard Law Rev.*, 30–70 (1926–1927).

66. William Blackstone, *Commentaries on the Laws of England*, 1st ed. (Oxford: Clarendon Press, 1765; reprint ed. Chicago: University of Chicago Press, 1979), vol. 1, p. 91.

67. Plucknett, "Bonham's Case and Judicial Review," pp. 63–68.

68. Clark, *History of the Royal College of Physicians*, vol. 1, p. 213.

69. Clark, *History of the Royal College of Physicians*, vol. 1, pp. 292–302.

70. Clark, *History of the Royal College of Physicians*, vol. 1, pp. 334–335.

71. Clark, *History of the Royal College of Physicians*, vol. 2, pp. 474–479.

72. Clark, *History of the Royal College of Physicians*, vol. 2, p. 514.

73. W. J. Reader, *Professional Men: The Rise of the Professional Classes in Nineteenth-Century England* (New York: Basic Books, 1966), pp. 16–18.

74. Reader, *Professional Men*, pp. 131–132.

75. *Professional Anecdotes* (London: John Knight and Henry Lacey, 1835), vol. 3, pp. 251–253.

76. Reader, *Professional Men*, pp. 42–43.

77. Clark, *History of the Royal College of Physicians*, vol. 3, p. 804.

78. Clark, *History of the Royal College of Physicians*, vol. 2, p. 558; vol. 3, p. 818.

79. "An Act to Regulate the Qualifications of Practitioners in Medicine and Surgery," *Statutes of the United Kingdom, 21 and 22 Victoria*, 1857–58, Cap. 40, 2 August 1858; pp. 299–312.

CHAPTER 5

1. It was none too soon. The conditions that moved the Bishop of London to action were to get worse before they got better. They were the conditions that Henry Mahew described so vividly a little later in *London Labour and London Poor* (London: Griffin, Bohn, 1861–1862; reprint ed. New York: Dover, 1968). See also Carleton B. Chapman, "The Year of the Great Stink," *The Pharos* 34:30–51 (January 1971).

2. J. Harley Williams, *A Century of Public Health in Britain, 1832–1929* (London: A. and C. Black, 1932), pp. 8–14. Chadwick was a devoted Benthamite and a barrister who "had not much faith in doctors, looked on them as necessary evils, and as not very likely to last." Benjamin Ward Richardson, *The Health of the Nations: A Review of the Works of Edwin Chadwick* (London: Dawson's of Pall Mall, 1965 [1887]), vol. 1, p. xvii. Thomas Southwood Smith was a Unitarian minister before he entered medicine and became ". . . one of the first doctors in this country to be turned aside from leeching, bleeding, and purging . . . into a scientific study of the causes of the disease" (Williams, p. 265). His medical degree, awarded in 1816, was from Edinburgh. He became licentiate of the Royal College in 1821 but was not made fellow until 1847. John Simon, K.C.B., obtained medical training at Kings College, London and moved rapidly into prominence in medical circles. His specialty was surgery and he never sought admission to London's Royal College of Physicians. He was elected to the Royal Society in 1855, when he was only 39, and was a prime mover in protecting the health of

Britain's millions until he resigned from public service in 1876. See generally G. Kitson Clark, *The Making of Victorian England* (New York: Athenaeum, 1967), pp. 97–107.

3. E. J. Hobsbawm, *The Age of Revolution: 1789–1848* (New York: World Publishing, 1964), pp. 241–243.

4. See generally J. W. Gough, *The Social Contract: A Critical Study of Its Development* (Oxford: Clarendon Press, 1957). In the development of a theory of profession, an analogue of the social contract theory was current at least as early as the eighteenth century: physicians through their guilds claimed some of the rights of government plus special economic privileges; they, in turn, were expected to place the patient's interests and rights paramount, within the professional relationship. Social contract as a political theory has today ceased to have much relevance, but its analogue as applied to the professions, especially medicine and law, is still of interest.

5. Harold L. Wilensky, "The Professionalization of Everyone," *Amer. J. Sociol.* 70:137–158 (September 1964).

6. Wilensky, "Professionalization of Everyone," p. 145.

7. Michael Garceau, "The Morals of Medicine," *Ann. Amer. Acad. Political and Social Sci.* 363:60–69 (January 1966).

8. Percival nevertheless knew and was respected by many of the College's more illustrious members and was invited, about 1775, to apply for membership. He never got around to doing so. See George Clark, *History of the Royal College of Physicians of London* (Oxford: Clarendon Press, 1966), vol. 2, p. 613.

9. Chauncey D. Leake, *Percival's Medical Ethics* (Baltimore: Williams and Wilkins, 1927; reprint ed. with additional material, Huntington, N.Y.: Robert Krieger, 1975), pp. 25–29. Also Edward M. Brockbank, *Sketches of the Lives and Work of the Honorary Staff of the Manchester Infirmary* (Manchester: University Press, 1904), pp. 53–107.

10. Leake, *Percival's Medical Ethics*, p. 65. The words are Percival's own, taken from his preface. The full title of his magnum opus is *Medical Ethics; or a code of institutes and precepts adapted to the professional conduct of physicians and surgeons* (Manchester: S. Russell, 1803).

11. *Of Professional Conduct Relative to Hospitals. . . .*

12. Leake, *Percival's Medical Ethics*, p. xxx. Emphasis Leake's.

13. Leake, *Percival's Medical Ethics*, pp. 68–69. Percival, *Medical Ethics*, p. 6.

14. Clark, *History of the Royal College of Physicians*, vol. 2, pp. 558–559.

15. Oxford: John Parker, 1847.

16. Thomas Gisborne, *An Enquiry into the Duties of Men in the Higher and Middle Classes of Society in Great Britain, Resulting from Their Respective Sta-*

tions, Professions, and Employments (London: J. David, 1794). Chapter twelve is entitled "On the Duties of Physicians Resulting from their Profession." This chapter was reprinted with the same title by John Henry Parker, Oxford, 1847. The original work is a commentary on the social structure of Britain in the late eighteenth century. Starting with the sovereign, Gisborne runs through the upper social strata, describing the ethical obligation of each, largely in terms that reflect the thinking of philosophers of the latter decades of the Enlightenment.

17. Gisborne, *Enquiry into the Duties of Men*, p. 396 of the original work; pp. 18–19 of the Oxford reprint.

18. Gisborne, *Enquiry into the Duties of Men*, pp. 400 and 404 of the original work; pp. 24 and 29 of the Oxford reprint.

19. John Gregory, *Observations on the Duties and Offices of a Physician and on the Method of Prosecuting Enquiries in Philosophy* (London: W. Strahan and T. Cadell, 1770), pp. 39–40.

20. Leake, *Percival's Medical Ethics*, p. 68; Percival, *Medical Ethics*, p. 6.

21. Leake, *Percival's Medical Ethics*, p. 71; Percival, *Medical Ethics*, p. 9. Emphasis Percival's.

22. Leake, *Percival's Medical Ethics*, p. 90; Percival, *Medical Ethics*, p. 30.

23. Leake, *Percival's Medical Ethics*, p. 104; Percival, *Medical Ethics*, p. 46.

24. Association of Boston Physicians, "Boston Medical Police" (Boston: Snelling and Simons, 1808).

25. Association of Boston Physicians, "Boston Medical Police," p. 8.

26. *Trans. Med. Soc. State of New York, 1807–1831* (Albany: van Benthuysen and Sons, 1868), pp. 231–245.

27. *Trans. Med. Soc. State of New York*, p. 236. Some twenty years earlier, Max Simon, a French physician, published *Déontologie médicale, ou des devoirs et des droits des médecins dans l'état actuel de la civilisation* (Paris: J. B. Baillière, 1845). Simon's emphases were somewhat similar to those adopted by the New Yorkers in their *Specifications of Medical Ethics in Practice*. Simon, however, wrote at great length, and devoted his Book Two to the physician's duties to his patients. Book Four was concerned with the rights of the physician. In spirit, he seems to have been closer to Caius than to Gisborne.

28. *Trans. Med. Soc. State of New York*, p. 243.

29. Medico-Chirurgical Society of Baltimore, *A System of Medical Ethics* (Baltimore: Lucas and Deaver, 1832).

30. Medico-Chirurgical Society of Baltimore, *System of Medical Ethics*, p. 14.

31. Michael Ryan, *A Manual of Medical Jurisprudence*, 1st American ed. (Philadelphia: Carey and Lea, 1832).

32. Ryan, *Manual of Medical Jurisprudence*, pp. 51–53.

33. Worthington Hooker, *Physician and Patient* (New York: Baker and Scribner, 1849).

34. Moshe Silberg, *Talmudic Law and the Modern State* (New York: Burning Bush Press, 1973), pp. 61–62.

35. Richard A. Posner, "A Theory of Negligence," *Legal Studies* 1:29–96 (January 1972).

36. John G. Fleming, "The Role of Negligence in Modern Tort Law," *Virginia Law Rev.* 53:815–846 (1967). Charles O. Gregory, "Trespass to Negligence to Absolute Liability," *Virginia Law Rev.* 37:359–375 (1951). Percy H. Winfield, "The History of Negligence in the Law of Torts," *Law Quart. Rev.* 42:184–201 (April 1926). Elizabeth Jean Dix, "The Origins of the Action of Trespass on the Case," *Yale Law J.* 46:1142–1176 (1937).

37. Anthony Fitzherbert, *The New Natura Brevia*, 9th ed. (London: Straham and W. Woodfall, 1794), vol. 1, 94D. The original edition appeared in 1534.

38. *The Colonial Laws of Massachusetts. Reprinted from the Edition of 1672*, William H. Whitmore, Supervisor (Boston: City Council, 1887), p. 28. The statute was added to Massachusetts Colonial law in 1649.

39. William Blackstone, *Commentaries on the Laws of England*, 10th ed. (London: A. Straham and T. Caddel, 1787), vol. 3, p. 122. The tenth edition is said to have been the last to be edited by Blackstone himself. The first edition is now available in facsimile (Chicago: University of Chicago Press, 1979). There are many American editions, the last, an incomplete one, being that published by Boston's Beacon Press in 1962.

40. *Dr. Groenvelt's case, 1 Lord Raymond*, 213–214 (1694).

41. The earliest use of the word malpractice seems to have been by Maynwaring, a seventeenth-century apothecary who used it in an attack on the "multitude of professors" (Fellows of the Royal College of Physicians) in *Praxis medicorum* (London: J. M. [T. Archer] 1671). The author uses the word *male-Practice* on page 2. He goes on to say that "'Tis medicine cures, not learned talk" and (p. 95) chides the physicians for forbidding their members to prepare their own medicaments.

42. *Cross v. Guthrie, 1 Amer. Dec.* 61–62 (1794).

43. The second case was *Grannis v. Brandon (5 Amer. Dec.* 143–148, 1812), and the third was *Landon v. Humphrey (9 Day Rep.* 209–216, 1832).

44. *Commonwealth v. Thompson, 6 Tyng Rep.*, 134–142 (1809).

45. *Sumner v. Utley, 7 Day Rep.* 257–266 (1828). At p. 263.

46. *Landon v. Humphrey, 9 Day Rep.* 209 (1834).

47. *Leighton v. Sargent, 7 Foster,* 460–476 (1853).

48. *McCandless v. McWha, 22 Penna.* 261–274 (1853).

49. That a physician does not guarantee a cure, but "undertakes to bring

a fair, reasonable and competent degree of skill and care" were opinions brought into English common law by Nicolas Conyngham Tyndal, Chief Justice of Common Pleas, in two cases: *Hancke v. Hooper, 173 Eng. Rep.*, 37–38 (1835), and *Lamphir and Wife v. Phipos, 173 Eng. Rep.* 581–583 (1838). In American law, the statement defining the physician's legal obligation to his patient by Justice Vann in *Pike v. Honsinger (49 NE, 760, 1896, at p. 762)* is often cited.

50. Blackstone, *Commentaries*, vol. 3, p. 117.

51. James Kent, *Commentaries on American Law* (New York: O. Halsted, 1826; facsimile ed., New York: Da Capo Press, 1971), vol. 1, p. 462.

52. Francis Hilliard, *The Law of Torts, or Private Wrongs* (Boston: Little, Brown, 1859).

53. But the number of medical malpractice actions grew very slowly. The late Hubert Smith found only twenty-three from 1794 to 1860; by 1900 his total was 217 and by 1940 it was 1,513. See his "Legal Responsibility for Medical Malpractice: IV. Malpractice Claims in the United States," *J. Amer. Med. Assoc.* 116:2670–2679 (1941). Sandor, using stricter criteria for definitions, found 1,936 cases of medical malpractice from 1794 to 1955; see *J. Amer. Med. Assoc.* 163:459–466 (1957). He estimated that for every case decided in appeals courts, about a hundred are actually filed. Joseph Stetler identified 605 appellate court decisions in medical malpractice cases for the twenty-year period 1935–1955; see *Temple Law Quart.* 30:355–386. It should be remembered, however, that the legal record includes only those cases that come to appeal. Actions that are tried but do not come to appeal are recorded locally but not nationally.

54. "An act for the constitution of a Supreme Court" (Judicature Act), *Pub. Gen. Stat., 36–37 Victoria*, 1873, chapt. 66, pp. 306–360. See also Alan Harding, *A Social History of English Law* (Harmondsworth: Penguin Books, 1966), pp. 330–339.

55. Simon Greenleaf, *A Treatise on the Law of Evidence*, 2nd ed. (Boston: Little, Brown, 1848), p. 74.

56. *Brown v. Kendall, 6 Cushing*, 292–298 (1850), at pp. 296 and 298. Shaw grew up on Cape Cod and graduated Harvard College, class of 1800. He received his legal training as an apprentice in a Boston law office. Harvard's law school was not founded until 1817.

57. Thomas E. Shearman and Amasa A. Redfield, *A Treatise on the Law of Negligence*, 2nd ed. (New York: Baker, Voorhis, 1870), pp. 504–513.

58. Shaw ultimately used three legal devices, termed the "unholy trinity" by John Fleming in "The Role of Negligence in Modern Tort Law," *Virginia Law Rev.* 53:815–846 (1967): The fellow servant rule (a manufacturer was not liable for the negligent acts of employees that caused injury to fellow employees); the assumption of risk rule (an employee entering on

an occupation he knows to be dangerous assumes liability for injury himself); and the contributory negligence rule (if the employee's negligence causes or contributes to the mishap, the employer is not liable). See also Morton J. Horwitz, *The Transformation of American Law, 1788–1860* (Cambridge: Harvard University Press, 1977), pp. 63–108.

59. The principles involved were validated by the U.S. Supreme Court in *New York Central Railroad Company v. White, 243 U.S. Rep.* 188–209 (1916). See also Charles O. Gregory, "Trespass to Negligence to Absolute Liability," *Virginia Law Rev.* 37:359–397.

60. Walter F. Dodd, *Administration of Workmen's Compensation* (New York: Commonwealth Fund, 1936), pp. 2–3.

61. John Elwell, *A Medico-Legal Treatise on Malpractice and Medical Evidence* (New York: John S. Voorhis, 1860), p. 23.

62. *Tefft v. Wilcox, 6 Webb,* 46–65 (1870), at p. 63. See also *Small v. Howard, 128 Massachusetts. Rep.* 131–316 (1880).

63. Richard M. Marcus, "Conspiracy of Silence," *Cleveland-Marshall Law Review* 14:520–533 (September 1965). Joseph Kelner, "The Silent Doctors: The Conspiracy of Silence," *University of Richmond Law Rev.* 5:119–127 (Fall, 1970). Daria D. Armstrong, "Medical Malpractice: The Locality Rule and the Conspiracy of Silence," *South Carolina Law Rev.* 2:810–821 (1970). Anon "Overcoming the Conspiracy of Silence: Statutory and Common Law Innovations," *Minnesota Law Rev.* 45:1019–1950 (May 1961).

64. *Bernstein v. Alameda–Contra Costa County Medical Assoc.,* 293 P 2nd 862 (1956).

65. A change that began with *Rann v. Twitchell, 71 Atl. Rep.* 1045–1047 (1909).

66. *Brune v. Belinkoff, 534 Massachusetts Rep.* 102–110 (1968).

67. Cicero, *Orations: On Behalf of Titus Annius Milo,* 53 (LCL 252), pp. 64–65.

68. *Byrne v. Boadle, 159 Eng. Rep.* 299–301 (1863). Pollock's actual statement was: "There are certain cases of which it may be said res ipsa loquitur, and this seems one of them" (p. 300).

69. *Evan v. Munro, 83 Atl. Rep.* 82 (1912).

70. David S. Rubsamen, "Res Ipsa Loquitur in California Malpractice Law: Expansion of a Doctrine to the Bursting Point," *Stanford Law Rev.* 14:251–283 (1962), pp. 256–257.

71. Rubsamen, "Res Ipsa Loquitur," pp. 276–283.

72. Aaron J. Broder, "Res Ipsa Loquitur in Medical Malpractice Cases," *De Paul Law Rev.* 18:421–431 (1969), pp. 423–425. See also O. C. Adamson, "Medical Malpractice: Misuse of Res Ipsa Loquitur," *Minnesota Law Rev.* 46:1043–1057 (1962), p. 1043.

73. See generally Jon R. Waltz and Thomas W. Scheuneman, "Informed Consent to Therapy," *Northwestern Univ. Law Rev.* 64:628–650 (1969).

74. *Salgo v. Leland Stanford Jr. University Board of Trustees, 1954 Ca. 2nd* 560; 317 P 2nd 170 (1957).

75. Blackstone, *Commentaries*, book 1, chapt. 1.

76. Blackstone, *Commentaries*, book 3, chapt. 8, p. 120.

77. *Beach v. Hancock, 7 Foster* (New Hampshire) 223–237 (1855), p. 229.

78. For example, Thomas M. Cooley, *On the Law of Torts, or the Wrongs which Arise Independent of Contract* (Chicago: Callaghan and Company, 1879). At p. 29 the author says: "The right to one's person may be said to be a right of complete immunity: to be let alone."

79. John Stuart Mill, *On Liberty* (1859), in *Utilitarianism, On Liberty, Essay on Bentham*, ed. Mary Warnock (New York: Meridian Books, 1962), p. 135.

80. *Pratt v. Davis, 118 Illinois* 161–184 (1905), pp. 166–167. See also *Central Law J.* 60:452–453 (1905).

81. *Mather v. Williams, 95 Minn.* 261–271 (1905). The court cited *Pratt v. Davis* and other authorities, and concluded that "the act of the defendant amounted at least to a technical assault and battery" (p. 271).

82. *Schloendorff v. New York Hospital, 211 New York* 125–135 (1914), pp. 129–130. Where private property is concerned the right to privacy goes back at least to *Semayne's Case 5 Coke Rep. 91a; Kings Bench, Mich. Term, 2 Jac I* (1605), in vol. 3, p. 185 of the Butterworth edition (1826). It contains the principle: "That the house of every one is to him as his castle and fortress . . ." (p. 186). See also "Note: The Right to Privacy in Nineteenth-Century America," *Harvard Law Rev.* 94:1892 (June 1981). The related principle, the right to privacy, was the subject of an important paper by Samuel Warren and Louis D. Brandeis, *Harvard Law Rev.* 4:193 (15 December 1890). The key phrase came from Cooley, *On the Law of Torts.* A constitutional right to be let alone was inferred from the Bill of Rights in *Griswold v. Connecticut 381 U.S.* 479 (1965), pp. 484–486.

83. *Natanson v. Kline, 186 Kans. Rep.* 393–414 (1960); 350 P 2d, 1093–1103 (1960). Also *Canterbury v. Spence,* 464 F 2d, 772–292 (1972).

CHAPTER 6

1. Charles M. Andrews, *The Colonial Period of American History, Vol. 1, The Settlement* (New Haven: Yale University Press, 1964 [1934]), pp. 270–271.

2. Richard H. Shryock, *Medical Licensing in America, 1650–1965* (Baltimore: Johns Hopkins Press, 1961), p. 15. See also Henry Burnell Shafer, *The American Medical Profession, 1783–1850* (New York: Columbia University Press, 1936), pp. 21–22.

3. Shafer, *American Medical Profession*, p. 22.

4. Shryock, *Medical Licensing in America*, p. 23.

5. Shryock, *Medical Licensing in America*, pp. 30–31.

6. A. M. Carr-Sanders and P. A. Wilson: *The Professions* (Oxford: Clarendon Press, 1933), p. 71. The authors quote Neil Arnott, "Report of the Select Committee on Medical Education," (1834) part 1, p. 94.

7. Donald E. Konold, *A History of American Medical Ethics, 1847–1917* (Madison: Department of History, University of Wisconsin, 1962), p. 1. See also Francis R. Packard, *The History of Medicine in the United States* (Philadelphia: J. P. Lippincott, 1901), chapt. 8, pp. 375–428.

8. Morris Fishbein, *A History of the American Medical Association* (Philadelphia: W. B. Saunders, 1947), pp. 6–7.

9. *Proceedings of the National Medical Conventions Held in New York, May 1846, and in Philadelphia, May 1847* (Philadelphia: T. K. and K. P. Collins, Printers, 1847), p. 17. The title American Medical Association and the establishment of constituent societies at state and county levels were accepted at the Philadelphia meeting in 1847.

10. *Proceedings*, p. 17.

11. *Proceedings*, pp. 86–87.

12. *Proceedings*, p. 90.

13. *Proceedings*, p. 92.

14. *Proceedings*, p. 93.

15. *Proceedings*, p. 97.

16. *Proceedings*, p. 100.

17. *Proceedings*, p. 106.

18. *Proceedings*, p. 106.

19. *Proceedings*, p. 93.

20. *Proceedings*, p. 105.

21. *Trans.Amer.Med. Assoc.* 8:56–57, 1855.

22. *Trans. Amer. Med. Assoc.* 9:59–61, 1856.

23. *Trans. Amer. Med. Assoc.* 11:70–71, 1858.

24. "Editorial," *J. Amer. Med. Assoc.* 6:155–157 (6 February 1886).

25. E. H. Bowman, "Medical Ethics," *J. Amer. Med. Assoc.* 2:540–544 (May 1884).

26. "Editorial: Medical Etiquette," *The Nation* 3:54–55 (19 July 1866).

27. Fishbein, *History of the AMA*, p. 153.

28. *J. Amer. Med. Assoc.* 38:1649–1652 (21 June 1902). See also *New York State J. Med.* 2:193 (June 1902).

29. *J. Amer. Med. Assoc.* 40:1379–1381 (16 May 1903).

30. Donald Konold, *History of American Medical Ethics*, p. 69. See also *J. Amer. Med. Assoc.* 40:1379 (16 May 1903).

31. *J. Amer. Med. Assoc.* 40:1379 (16 May 1903).

32. *J. Amer. Med. Assoc.* 40:1380 (16 May 1903).

33. AMA policy strongly favored government intervention in matters

concerning the health of the millions, but it sternly forbade government involvement when the consideration was personal health services. See generally Carleton B. Chapman and John M. Talmadge, "Historical and Political Background of Federal Health and Legislation," *Law and Contemporary Problems: Health Care, Part I* (Durham: Duke University School of Law, Spring 1970).

34. *J. Amer. Med. Assoc.* 58:1789–1793 (8 June 1912). Adopted 4 June; see *J. Amer. Med. Assoc.* 58:1907 (15 June 1912).

35. *J. Amer. Med. Assoc.* 58:1793 (8 June 1912).

36. "Minutes of the House of Delegates, 27 April," *J. Amer. Med. Assoc.* 74:1319 (8 May 1920). "Minutes of the House of Delegates, 25 May 1922," *J. Amer. Med. Assoc.* 78:1715 (3 June 1922). See generally Carleton B. Chapman and John M. Talmadge, "The Evolution of the Right to Health Concept in the United States," *Pharos* 34:50–51 (January 1971).

37. Fishbein, *History of AMA*, pp. 951–960.

38. Richard C. Cabot, "Ethics and the Medical Profession," *The Survey* 55:618–643 (1 March 1926). See also Thomas Franklin Williams, "Cabot, Peabody, and the Care of the Patient," *Bull. Hist. Med.* 24:462–481 (Sept.– Oct. 1950).

39. Cabot, "Ethics and the Medical Profession," p. 643.

40. Cabot, "Ethics and the Medical Profession," p. 620.

41. F. W. Peabody, "The Care of the Patient," *J. Amer. Med. Assoc.* 88:877–882 (19 March 1927). Also published in book form (Cambridge: Harvard University Press, 1927).

42. Peabody, "Care of the Patient," p. 877. Italics added. Also published separately in *Doctor and Patient* (New York: Macmillan, 1930), pp. 27–57.

43. Peabody, "Care of the Patient," p. 877.

44. Peabody, "Care of the Patient," p. 879.

45. The defendants (the AMA and the District of Columbia Medical Society) were found guilty on 14 April 1941. See Fishbein, *History of the AMA*, pp. 534–550. See also *United States v. American Medical Association et al.*, 110 F. 2nd, 703–716 (1940); *American Medical Assoc. v. United States*, 317 US, 536 (1943). The entire episode is set out impartially by K. L. Pullar and R. E. Pumphrey, "The Anti-Trust Suit Against the AMA, 1939– 1943," *Social Work in Health Care* 3:287–296 (Spring 1978).

46. "Minutes of House of Delegates, 1 December 1948," *J. Amer. Med. Assoc.* 138:1241 (25 December 1948). "Address to the House of Delegates by Leon Baxter," *J. Amer. Med. Assoc.* 140:694–696 (25 June 1949).

47. Milton Mayer, "The Dogged Retreat of the Doctors," *Harper's* 199:25– 37 (December 1949). See also *J. Amer. Med. Assoc.* 156:1514 (18 December 1954). The mood of Congress vis-à-vis the AMA had been reflected a few

years earlier when a member of the House noted that ". . . the only kind of medical aid bill the AMA would approve is a measure which would place unlimited public funds in the hands of the AMA itself, to dispense as it sees fit after paying lobbying and propaganda expenses. . . ." Andrew Biemiller, 81st Cong., 2nd Sess., *Cong. Rec.* 96:(10):13904 (30 August 1950).

48. *J. Amer. Med. Assoc.* 140:700–703 (25 June 1949).

49. *J. Amer. Med. Assoc.* 140, p. 700.

50. *J. Amer. Med. Assoc.*, 140, p. 701.

51. *J. Amer. Med. Assoc.* 159:1754–1756 (31 December 1955).

52. *J. Amer. Med. Assoc.* 162:504–505 (29 September 1956).

53. *J. Amer. Med. Assoc.* 164:886 (22 June 1957).

54. *Opinions and Reports of the Judicial Council* (Chicago: American Medical Association, 1971), p. iv.

55. Robert Reinhold, "AMA, Facing Legal Pressures, Adopts Less Rigid Code for Doctors," *New York Times*, 23 July 1980.

56. "A physician should practice a method of healing founded on a scientific basis; and he should not voluntarily associate professionally with anyone who violates this principle."

57. Robert M. Veatch, "Professional Ethics: New Principles for Physicians?" *Hastings Center Rep.* 10:16–19 (June 1980).

58. Veatch, "Professional Ethics," p. 19.

59. P. Caws, "On the Teaching of Ethics in a Pluralistic Society," *Hastings Center Rep.* 8(5):32–39 (1978).

60. Veatch, "Professional Ethics," p. 19.

61. Judith Swazey, *Health, Professionals, and the Public: Toward a New Social Contract?* (Philadelphia: Society for Health and Human Values, 1979), p. 24.

62. A. R. Jonsen, *The Rights of Physicians: A Philosophical Essay* (Washington, D.C.: Institute of Medicine, 1978), p. 26.

CHAPTER 7

1. Robert Nisbet, *History of the Idea of Progress* (New York: Basic Books, 1980), p. 6. Italics added.

2. Hippocrates, Law I, 4–7 (LCL 148), pp. 262–263.

3. Carleton B. Chapman, "Doctors and Their Autonomy: Past Events and Future Prospects," *Science* 200:851–856 (26 May 1978).

4. Probably beginning with *Pelky v. Palmer*, 109 Mich. 561 (1896). See also Jon R. Waltz, "The Rise and Gradual Fall of the Locality Rule in Medical Malpractive Litigation," *De Paul Law Rev.* 18:408 (1969).

5. Richard E. Simpson, "Informed Consent: From Disclosure to Patient

Participation in Medical Decisionmaking," *Northwestern University Law Rev.* 76:172 (1981).

6. *Helling v. Carey*, 519 P. 2d 981 (1974).

7. Plato, *The Statesman* 298 A-302 B (LCL 164), pp. 147–161. See also Alexander Gould, "Wiser than the Laws? The Legal Accountability of the Medical Profession," *Amer. J. Law and Med.* 7:145–181 (Summer 1981).

8. Computer diagnosis of medical problems cannot be far off. Jurists have already begun to ponder the questions courts will face if and when a patient sustains injury that is adjudged to be the fault of a computer. The preliminary view is that computer programs will be treated as products (and thus come under the product liability heading) instead of as fallible, flesh-and-blood physicians. See generally Vincent M. Brannigan and Ruth E. Dayhoff, "Liability for Personal Injury Caused by Defective Medical Computer Programs," *Amer. J. Law and Med.* 7:123–145 (Summer 1981).

9. Charles O. Gregory, "Trespass to Negligence to Absolute Liability," *Virginia Law Rev.* 37:359 (April 1951). More recently, W. B. Schwartz and N. R. Konesar, in *Doctors, Damages, and Deterrence: An Economic View of Medical Malpractice* (Santa Monica: Rand Report R-2340-NIH/RC, June 1978), cited probable disadvantages to abandoning the tort system in the field of medical malpractice. Nonetheless, the concept of strict, or absolute, liability in tort is firmly entrenched in American law. See William L. Prosser, *Law of Torts*, 4th ed. (St. Paul: West, 1971), pp. 657–658. In Prosser's words, "The courts have . . . recognized a new doctrine that the defendant's enterprise, while it will be tolerated by law, must pay its [own] way" (p. 494).

10. Richard A. Abel, "Torts," in *The Politics of Law*, ed. David Kairys (New York: Pantheon, 1982), p. 199.

11. "Jury Awards Girl $29.9 Million," *New York Times*, 2 October 1982. See also W. Oster, "Medical Malpractice Insurance," *Insurance Council J.* 45:228–236 (April 1978). Oster's estimate is that only 27 percent of premiums paid for malpractice insurance is paid out in awards to patients; the average time from injury to payout was 6.5 years in 1978 (pp. 229–230).

12. Prosser, *Law of Torts*, p. 509.

13. Geoffrey Palmer, *Compensation for Incapacity* (Wellington: Oxford University Press, 1979), p. 56. Italics added. An article by a New Zealand lawyer, D. R. Harris, detailing the faults of the fault system and titled "The Law of Torts and the Welfare State," *New Zealand Law J.* 1963:171–84 (June), was apparently influential in initiating the movement.

14. *Compensation for Personal Injury in New Zealand*, Report of the Royal Commission of Injury (Woodhouse Report) (Wellington: December 1967), p. 20. Italics added. See generally: *A Brief Description of the Accident Com-*

pensation Scheme Operating in New Zealand (Wellington: Accident Compensation Commission, 1976).

15. I. I. Kosarev, "Evolution of the Medical Ethical Code in the U.S.S.R. and abroad," *Vest. Akad. Med. Nauk.*, *S.S.R.* 1980:47–52 (No. 4). It is not, however, very simple to discern the place of ethics, professional or otherwise, in the Soviet Union. The Webbs, nearly fifty years ago, were almost convinced that ". . . Soviet Communism . . . is, in morals as well as in economics and political science, actually leading the world." Sidney Webb and Beatrice Webb, *Soviet Communism: A New Civilization:* (New York: Charles Scribner's Sons, 1936), p. 1134. More recently George C. Guins wrote that in the Western world ". . . a philosophy of law reflects inevitably the prevailing ethical principles and social trends. . . . At the same time moral principles, backed mainly [but not entirely] by religious sanctions, are more general and more impressive than the law. . . . All this is foreign to the ethical philosophy of Communism in its Soviet interpretation." It is, Guins points out, standard Marxism to assume that "existing moral systems" are tools of the dominant class in any society, and that capitalist society uses both justice and morals for ". . . the exploitation of man by man." In the Soviet concept of ethics, conflicts between law and ethics are impossible. The function of both law and ethics is to place above all else the Communist program and to subordinate personal interests to those of the collective society. "The highest authority belongs to Communist policy and the party line, and ethics gets its principles and criteria from that source." To hate the enemies of the Soviet state and to avenge all traitors ". . . is both a legal and moral duty for every Soviet citizen." See his *Soviet Law and Soviet Society* (The Hague: Martines Nijhoff, 1954), pp. 24–36. If Guins, who is plainly anti-Soviet, is correct, the Soviet physician is guided mainly by his all-encompassing obligation to the state; to place the patient's interests above all else is, thus, subversive or worse.

16. William Munk, *Euthanasia: or Medical Treatment in and of an Easy Death* (London: Longmans Green, 1887), p. 86.

17. John Ferriar, *Medical Histories and Reflections* (London: Cadell and David, 1798), vol. 3, p. 193. Ferriar was a contemporary and close friend of William Percival. See also E. M. Brockbank, *John Ferriar* (London: William Heineman, 1950).

18. Munk, *Euthanasia*, p. 74.

19. Henry Holland, *Medical Notes and Reflections* (London: Longman, Orme, Brown, Green, and Longmans, 1839), p. 419.

20. Alabama, Arkansas, California, Delaware, Idaho, Illinois, Kansas, Nevada, New Mexico, North Carolina, Oregon, Texas, Vermont, Washington, and the District of Columbia (as of mid-1983).

21. *In re Quinlan*, 70 N.J. 10 (1976).

22. *Eichner v. Dillon*, 426 N.Y.S. 2d 517 (1980). The New York Supreme Court, Appelate Division, in permitting discontinuance of life-sustaining measures in the case of Brother Joseph Fox, rested its decision on the common law right of bodily self-determination and not on the more controversial constitutional right to privacy. In so doing, the Court took note of the action in 1957 of Pope Pius XII to the effect that the use of "extraordinary means to prolong life" could be foregone under some circumstances. It also cited the Vatican's "Declaration on Euthanasia" of 1980.

23. *Eichner v. Dillon*, p. 542.

24. Donald G. Collester, "Death, Dying and the Law: A Prosecutional View of the Quinlan Case," *Rutgers Law Rev.* 30:304 (1976–1977). See also Dennis J. Horan, "Termination of Medical Treatment," *A.B.A. Forum* 16:470 (Winter 1981).

25. Stanford H. Kadish: "Respect for Life and Regard for Rights in the Criminal Law," in *Respect for Life in Medicine, Philosophy, and the Law* (Baltimore: Johns Hopkins University Press, 1975), p. 89.

26. Ian B. Thompson, "The Implications of Medical Ethics," *J. Med. Ethics* 2:74–84 (June 1976).

27. Cheryl N. Noble, et al., "Ethics and Experts," *Hastings Center Rep.* 12:7–17 (June 1982).

28. *Proceedings of the National Medical Conventions Held in New York, May 1846, and in Philadelphia, May 1847* (Philadelphia: T. K. and K. P. Collins, Printers, 1847), p. 17.

29. William Withey Gull, *A Collection of the Published Writings* (London: New Sydenham Society, 1896), pp. 37–38, and 119.

30. Huxley is quoted in "Editorial: On the Medical Curriculum," *Nature* 9:21–22 (13 November 1873).

31. Thomas H. Huxley, "Address on University Education," in *American Addresses* (New York: D. Appleton, 1877), p. 109.

32. Thomas H. Huxley, *Science and Education: Collected Essays* (New York: D. Appleton, 1898), vol. 3, p. 321. Also, "Letter to Professor Roy Lankester," in *Life and Letters of Thomas Henry Huxley*, ed. Leonard Huxley (London: Macmillan, 1900), vol. 2, pp. 309–310.

33. Ludwig Eichna, "Medical School Education, 1975–1979: A Student's Perspective," *New England J. Med.* 303:727–734 (25 September 1980).

34. Ronald Munson, "Why Medicine Cannot Be a Science," *J. Med. and Philosophy* 6:183–208 (May 1981).

35. George L. Engel, "The Biomedical Model: A Procrustian Bed?" *Man and Medicine* 4:257–275 (1979).

36. Munson, "Why Medicine Cannot Be a Science," p. 185.

37. Munson, "Why Medicine Cannot Be a Science," p. 194.

38. Edmund D. Pellegrino and David C. Thomsma, *A Philosophical Basis of Medical Practice* (New York: Oxford University Press, 1981), pp. 58–81.

39. In October 1957. The first manned space flight, also a Soviet achievement, took place on 12 April 1961.

40. G. Holton, "Science for Nonscientists: Criteria for College Programs," *Teachers College Record* 64:497–509 (1962–63).

41. K. Danner Clouser, "What is Medical Ethics?" *Ann. Int. Med.* 80:657–660 (May 1974).

42. Alan H. Goldman, *The Moral Foundation of Professional Ethics* (Totowa, N.J.: Rowman and Littlefield, 1980), pp. 6–9, and 18.

43. Gerald J. Postema, "Moral Responsibility in Professional Ethics," *New York U. Law Rev.* 55:63 (April 1980).

44. Martin L. Norton, "Ethics in Medicine and Law: Standards and Conflicts," *Med. Trial Technique Quart.* 1980 Annual: 376.

45. Molière, *Le Malade Imaginaire*, in *The Plays of Molière*, trans. A. R. Waller (Edinburgh: John Grant, 1926), vol. 8 (1671–1673), pp. 281–284.

46. Janice G. Raymond, "Medicine as Patriarchal Religion," *J. Med. and Philosophy* 7:197–216 (May 1982).

Index

Abortion
    opposition in *Oath*, 23
    Roman law on, 45
    Visigothic law on, 45
Acland, Henry, 137
Adams, Francis
    on Hippocratic Corpus, 21
Adultery
    law of Gortyn, 28–30
    on Olympus, 30
Aethelbert
    composition for medical treat-
        ment, 50–51
Aethelred
    laws, 50
Agricola
    plans to invade Ireland, 49
    Tacitus on, 163*n*1
Alexander the Great,
    death (23 B.C.), 32
Alexandria, library
    Hippocratic Corpus assembled, 20
    and Greek scholarship, 32
    destruction of, 155*n*27
Alfred
    tables of compensation, 50
Amenemope (Amenemapt)
    relation to Hebraic ethics, 151*n*24
American Medical Association

principles of medical ethics, 116
    founding, 105–107
    purposes, 105
    court, medical, 110
    instructions to public, 110
    adoption of code, 107, 111
    "a law unto ourselves . . , above
        all law save the Divine," 111
    revisions of 1903 and 1912, 112–
        113
    opposition to federal health leg-
        islation, xiv, 118–119
    violation of Sherman antitrust act,
        118–119, 177*n*45
    ten principles to seven, 122–123
    charges of paternalism, 123
Amos
    prophecies, 9–10
    and Hebraic tradition, 14
    echo in Luke, 12:48, 145
Amundsen, Darrell,
    on negligence in Greek law, 30–
        31
Antiphon
    tetralogy, 30
Aphrodite
    and Ares, 30
Apollo
    father of Asklepius, 18

Apothecaries
  Spicers and Pepperers, Grocers'
    Company, 61
  conflict with Royal College of
    Physicians, 71–72
  revision of medical education, 71
Archagathus
  Greek surgeon in Rome, 36
Aristotle
  opposition to Athenian democ-
    racy, 17
  an Asklepiad, 18
  on Dracon's law of homicide, 28
  on physicians' liability, 32
  death of, 32
Asklepiadai
  physicians' guild, xv, 18
  temples, 19
  family monopoly, 24
Asklepius
  myths and cult, 18–19
  mention in Iliad, 18
  Pindar, Pausanias, and Appolo-
    dorus on, 18
  tribal aspects, 19
  in the Oath, 19
  god or hero, 154n20
Athens
  Asklepiad temple, 19
  democracy, 16–17
Assyria
  laws of, 8
Authority, tradition of
  doctor to patient, and doctor to
    doctor, 140–141
  in Molière's Le Malade Imaginaire,
    141
  male homo-relational union, 141
  reinforcement by education, 142–
    143

Babylon,
  first dynasty, 3–4

exile (Hebraic), 14
Bacon, Francis
  on malpractice, 60
Baltimore
  Medico-Chirurgical Society, 87
Beach v. Hancock, 175n77
Bede, the Venerable
  on leeches and a physician, 61,
    166n31
Bell, John
  introduction to first AMA Code,
    106
Bentham, Jeremy
  and reform in Britain, 75
Bernstein v. Alameda–Contra Costa
    Medical Assoc., 174n64
Blackstone, William
  on malpractice, 92
Bonham, Thomas
  legal action against Royal College
    of Physicians, 69
  see also 168n65
Boston
  Medical Police, 86
  tradition of ethical role model, 118
Bracton, Henry de
  On the Laws and Customs of En-
    gland, 53
  Holdsworth on, 53
  on obligations, 53–54
  due care, 54
Breasted, James H.
  on Egyptian sources, 9
Brown v. Kendall, 173n56
Brune v. Belinkoff, 174n66
Bergundian code, 46
Bury, J. B.
  on Rome's decline, 44
Byzantium
  and Hellenism, 32

Cabot, Richard
  on medical ethics, 115–116

Caesar, Julius
  on Teutonic tribes and customs, 47
  special privileges to physicians, 38, 160*n*17
Caius, John
  compared to Linacre, 64–65
  Osler's view, 65
  on Galen, 65
  president of Royal College, 65
  and medical ethics, 66
Canterbury, Archbishop of
  awarding of medical degree, 63
Canterbury v. Spence, 175*n*83
Canute
  laws of, 50
Cato
  opposition to things Greek, 36
Cavendish, John
  in *Stratton v. Swanlond,* 57–59
  execution, 59
Caws, Peter
  on live ethical situations, 124
Celsus
  encyclopedist, 38
Chadwick, Edwin
  public health reform, 75
  ". . . not much faith in doctors," 169*n*2
Cheiron the Centaur
  teaches Asklepius, 18–19
Cicero
  De Officiis, on *ars,* 40
  stoicism, 40
  on *res ipsa loquitur,* 97–98
Clark, George
  historian of Royal College, 67
Clergy
  forbidden to practice medicine, 166*n*31
Clouser, K. D.
  medical ethics, 139–140
Clovis

retention of Roman law for Romans, 44
Coke, Edward
  opinion on Bonham's case, 69
  on conflict of interest, 73
Colonial law
  control of healers, 90
Common law
  precedent in, 52
  Bracton's influence, 53–55
  acceptance in America, 92, 94
Commonwealth v. Thompson, 172*n*44
Compensation
  for injury, 1
  in Anglo-Saxon law, 50–51
Corinth
  destruction by Rome, 35
Costs of health care, 146–147
Craftsman
  Greek concept, 25
Cynifrid, 61
Cross v. Guthrie, 172*n*42

Damages,
  Bracton on, 53–55
Daremberg, Charles Victor
  on *Oath,* 23
Davis, Nathan Smith
  founder of AMA, 105
Delictum
  in *lex Aquilia,* 37, 160*n*15
Delphi
  Asklepiad temple, 19
  Roman delegation to, 36
Denom's case
  early malpractice in common law, 55–56
Deodandum, 150*n*10
Dodd, Walter
  on Workmen's Compensation, 96
Dracon
  laws for Athens, 27–28
  on homicide, 28

Due care
  Bracton on, 54
  Cavendish definition, 59
Ecclesiasticus
  on physicians, 12–13
Edelstein, Ludwig and Emma
  Asklepiad studies, 18–19
  Oath and Pythagorean dogma, 23–25
  doubts, 24
Education
  Vitruvius on liberal, 39
  medical, need for revision, 147
  Huxley on, 136–137
  Gull on, 136
  and tradition of authority, 147
Edward the Confessor
  and Anglo-Saxon law, 51
Egypt
  and Hebrews, 9
Eichner v. Dillon, 181*n*22
Epidaurus
  Asklepiad temple, 19
  Roman delegation, 36
Erasmus
  association with Linacre, 62
Erotian
  earliest mention of *Oath*, 21
  list of authors writing about Hippocratic Corpus, 156*n*33
Eshnuna (Bilalama)
  monetary compensation, 3–4
  ox that gores, 4
Ethics
  beginnings, 1–2, 11
  and law, 2–3
  Sumerian and Babylonian, 3
  rules for rulers, 8
  and religion, 11
  interface with law, 88–89
  medical, opinions, 139–140
Evans v. Munro, 174*n*69

Fitzherbert
  definitions of negligence, 90
Fuchs, Robert
  on *Oath*, 23

Galen
  Greek origin, 38
  and medieval physicians, 61
  Caius' views on, 65
  Royal College and, 70
  no mention of *Oath*, 43
Gellius, Aulus
  definition of humanities, 161*n*32
Gibbon, Edward
  on Rome's decline, 43
Gisborne, Thomas
  on the duties of physicians, 81–82
Gortyn
  laws of, 28
Grannis v. Brandon, 172*n*43
Greece
  golden age, xv, 14–15
  archaic age, 14, 16
  tribes, 16
  city-states, 26
  law, 26–27, 56
Gregory, John
  "gentlemen of honour and ingenious manners," 83
Griswold v. Connecticut, 175*n*82
Grocers, 61
Grotius, Hugo, 160*n*13
Gull, William Henry
  on medicine and science, 136

Haephaestus,
  due fine of adultery, 30
Hammurabi
  laws of, 4–5
  and ethics, 5

Hancke v. Hooper, 172n49
Harvey, William
    Fellow of Royal College, 70–71
Hays, Isaac
    and AMA committee on ethics,
        106
    debt to Percival acknowledged,
        107
Haywood, Richard Mansfield
    on decline of Rome, 44
Helling v. Carey, 179n6
Henry II
    clash with Beckett, 55
Henry VIII
    and founding of Royal College, 62
Heschel, Abraham J.
    on justice and righteousness, 10–
        11
Hippocrates (see also *Oath* at-
        tributed to)
    descendant of Asklepius, 18
    Corpus, 19–20
    rejects supernatural, 20
    on absence of malpractice laws in
        Greece, 126
    lineage, 154n18
Hittite law, 8
Holton, Gerald
    on climbers and earthbound
        drudges, 139
Homer, 16
    Homeridai, xv
    probable dates, 16
    translation of epics into Latin, 34
Homicide
    Dracon's law, 28
    in Teutonic and early English law,
        47, 50
Hooker, Washington
    on professional conduct, 88
Horace
    on conquest of Rome by Greek
        culture, 35

Humanitas
    Scribonius on, 41
Huxley, Thomas
    on medical education and its ob-
        ject, 136–137
Iamidai
    prophet clan, xv
Iliad
    in writing, 14
    brutality in, 26
    trial scene, 27
Ine
    laws of, 50
Informed consent
    origins, 98–99
    J. S. Mill on, 99
    Benjamin Cardozo on, 99–100
Iniuria
    Roman concepts, 51
    Bracton on, 53–54
Isaiah I
    prophecies, 10
Jaspers, Karl
    axial period, 15
Jastrow, Morris
    on Sumerian healers, 7
Javanim
    (Greeks), Hebrew comments,
        153n3
Jeremiah
    prophecies of, 10
Johanan, Rabbi
    law and ethics, 12
Johns Hopkins University
    model for medical education, 136–
        137
Jones, W. H. S.
    on Hippocratic Corpus, 20
    on *Oath*, 21–22
Justinian
    closes Athens' schools of philos-
        ophy, 34

Justinian *(Continued)*
  Digest, rediscovery of, 52
  precepts of the law, 152*n*29

Kos
  Hippocrates' birthplace, 19
Kosarev, I. I., *see* Soviet Union
Kramer, Samuel Noah
  on Sumer, 5

Lamphir and Wife v. Phipos, 172*n*49
Landon v. Humphrey, 172*n*43
Leake, Chauncey
  on Percival's *Medical Ethics*, 80
Leges Henrici Primi
  in pre-conquest England, 53
Leighton v. Sargent, 172*n*47
Liability, strict
  in Workmen's Compensation, 100
  Charles Gregory on, 128–129
Licensure (medical)
  in the United States, 104–105
Linacre, Thomas
  origins and education, 62
  founder of Royal College of Physicians, 63
Lipit-Ishtar (1934–1924 B.C.)
  on ethics, 3
Littré, E.
  on the *Oath*, 21
Locality rule
  rise and fall, 96–97
Locke, John
  emphasis on observation, 71
Locrians
  legendary lawgivers, 27
Lombard laws
  after Rome's fall, 46
London, Bishop of
  role in licensing physicians, 63
  proposal concerning London's laboring poor, 75

Luke the Apostle
  "for unto whomsoever much is given . . ." xvi, 145

Macdowell, Douglas
  on Greek law, 28
Machaon
  son of Asklepius, 18
Maimonides
  Mishneh Torah, 14, 153*n*43
Malfeasance, 59
Malpractice
  in laws of Hammurabi, 4–5
  early cases in common law, 55–58
  lineage in common law, 60, 166*n*28
  purpose of law, 89
  Greek views, 89
  protective device for physicians, 126
  insurance premiums, 126–127
  defects, 129
  word coined, 172*n*41
  first American case, 92
  required degree of skill, 94
  increase in number of cases, 173*n*53
  crisis, 101
  court sets its own standards, 127
March, Alden
  founder of AMA, 105
Mather v. Williams, 175*n*81
Mayflower
  physicians aboard, 103
McCandless v. McWha, 172*n*48
Medical Act of 1858 (Great Britian)
  control of education and licensure, 73, 75, 104
Medicare-Medicaid

more fee for less service, xvi, 146–147

Medicine, identity
  Acland, Gull, and Huxley on, 137
  range of modern views, 138
  humanities and science; need for definitions, 147

Micah
  "what doth the Lord require of thee?" 11

Misfeasance, 59

Moses
  reception of decalogue, 7

Mycenae
  setting for epics, 16

Nanshe
  Sumerian goddess of ethics, 5

Natanson v. Kline, 175*n*83

National health insurance
  amendments proposed (1943–1965), 149*n*2 (introduction)

Negligence
  Bracton on, 54
  in Roman law, 54
  common law definitions, 2, 90–92
  peshiah in Talmudic law, 13

New Jersey
  first state medical association, 103

New York
  Medical Society of the State of, ethics, 86–87
  no obligation to inform patients, 87

New York Central Railroad Company v. White, 174*n*59

New Zealand
  abolishes tort system, 130
  Woodhouse comments, 130

Nittis, Saris
  opinion on *Oath*, 21–23

Nonfeasance, 59

Normans
  conquest, 51–52
  centralization of authority, 52

Norton, Martin L.
  medicine's ethical principle, 140

Oath attributed to Hippocrates, xiv, 20–23, 25
  Scribonius' comment, 21
  Edelstein's views, 22–24
  and Royal College of Physicians, 67
  English versions, 67

Odysseus
  slaughter of Penelope's suitors, 26–27, 29–30

Ostrogoths
  and Roman law, 44–45

Ox that gores, 4, 150*n*10

Peabody, Francis
  care of the patient, 116–117

Peasant's revolt
  "death to all lawyers. . . ." 59

Peer judgment
  Aristotle on, 31

Pelky v. Palmer, 178*n*4

Pellegrino, Edward, 138–139

Percival, Thomas
  life of, 78–80
  rules of professional conduct, 80
  use of *Statuta Moralia*, 80–81
  on Gisborne and Gregory, 81
  summary of *Medical Ethics*, 83–84
  patients to be kept in ignorance, 84
  Powers, Privileges, and Employments of the Faculty, 86

Pergamum
  Asklepian temple, 19

Pericles,
  funeral oration, 16–17
Philosophers
  relations with physicians, 133–134
Physicians
  position in Jewish society, 12–13
  Talmudic law on liability for
    damages, 13
  craftsmen in Greece, 25
Pike v. Honsinger, 172*n*49
Plato
  opposition to Athenian democ-
    racy, 17
  on physicians' liability, 31
  on laymen and professional stan-
    dards, 127
  on slavery, 154*n*13
Pliny the Edler
  on Greek physicians, 36
Plutarch
  on Dracon, 27
Podaleirus
  son of Asklepius, 18
Popper, Karl
  on Plato, Aristotle, Greek tribal-
    ism, 17
Pratt v. Davis, 175*n*80
Precedent
  in early common law, 52
Profession
  theory of, 8
  ethical obligations, 12
  Greek views, 25–26
  Scribonius and *professio*, 40
  service ideal (Wilensky), 77
  codes focusing on profession, 77
  stratification, 7
  Cicero on *ars*, 40
Prophets
  pre-exilic, 8–9
Public Health Act of 1848 (Great
  Britain), 75
Pythagoreans, *see* Edelstein

Quintillian
  on lawyers, 38
Rab
  law and ethics, 12
Res ipsa loquitur
  Pollock on, 98
  Cicero's coinage, 97–98
  enters American law, 98
  use to overcome "conspiracy of
    silence," 98
Revenge, *see* Talion and Self-help
Right to die
  derivative old right to be left
    alone, 131
  nineteenth-century British clini-
    cians on, 131–132
  natural death laws, 132
  positive and passive euthanasia,
    132–133
Righteousness and justice
  Sumerian concept, 3
  Hebraic principle, 10–11
Ritter, Edith K.
  on stratification of Sumerian
    healers, 7
Rome
  silver age, 33
  twelve tables, 35–36
  lex Aquilia, damage to slaves, 37,
    160*n*17
  law and abortion, 45
  Asklepiad temple, 36
  physicians' privileges, 37, 160*n*17
  education, 38
  guilds, 42
  in Britain, 50
  achievements compared to those
    of Greece, 38
Royal College of Physicians (London)
  founding, 63
  censors, 64

statutes penal or ethical, 66
court, 69
Bonham case, 69–70
Greek, Latin and Euclid, 71
and Oxbridge, 72
and noblesse oblige, 76–77

Schloendorff v. New York Hospital, 175*n*82
Scribonius Largus
on *professio*, 39–41
Self-help
modification in ancient law, 8
and trial scene in Iliad, 27
control in Anglo-Saxon law, 50
abolition in Dracon's law, 28
Semayne's Case, 175*n*82
Seneca
on physicians (in *De Beneficiis*), 41–42
Shaw, George Bernard, 146
Shaw, Lemuel
no liability without fault, 95, 173*n*58
Shulan Uruk
authority of, 153*n*43
Simon, John
public health in Britain, 75, 169*n*2
Simon, Max
Déontologie médicale, 171*n*27
Slavery
Plato on, 154*n*13
rights of slaves to medical care, 31
Social contract
and duties of professionals, 170*n*4
Solon
laws, 16
revision of Dracon's laws, 27–28
Roman delegation to, 34
Soviet Union
medical ethics on, 130–131
criticism of western codes, 131, 180*n*15

Stoics
Cicero and, 40
on medical humanism, 42
Seneca on, 41
Strabo
on earliest Greek law, 27
Stratton v. Swanlond (The Surgeon's Case of 1375), 57–59
Swazey, Judith
on social contract, 124
Sydenham, Thomas
and London's Royal College, 70–71

Tacitus
on Teutonic law, 46–47
Talion
law of, 8
replacement in Visigothic law, 45–46
definition in Exodus, 151*n*19
Talmud
and ethics, 12
law and negligence, 13
Techne
art and craft, 25, 40
Tefft v. Wilcox, 174*n*62
Teutons
law according to Tacitus, 46–47
Caesar on, 47
invasion of Britain, 50
Thomson, George
on origins of *Oath*, 23
Tonsillectomy, routine, 142
Tort law
analogues in ancient law, 1–2
Roman law and, 37
Blackstone on, 94
not mentioned by Kent, 94
Tosephta, 152*n*39
Trespass
Bracton on, 54

Trespass *(Continued)*
  and malpractice, 55
  Blackstone, 92
Troy
  fall, 16
Tyndall, Chief Justice
  definition of professional standards, 172*n*49

Ullmann, Walter
  ascending and descending government, 2, 150*n*4
United States v. American Medical Association, et al, 177*n*45
Updike, John
  on ethical standards of artists, 152*n*29
Urnammu
  monetary compensation in Sumer, 3
Urukagina of Lagash
  rulers' ethics, 2–3

Veatch, Robert
  on paternalism, 123
Vespasian
  edict on *medici*, 42
Visigoths
  laws, 44–46
  laws relating to physicians, 44–45

compensation substituted for talion, 45–46
Vitruvius
  on liberal education, 39

Warner versus Leech (1330), 56–57
Wergeld
  in Visigothic law, 45–46
  in early English law, 50–51
  absent in Bracton, 53
Westminster Hall
  greatest achievement of Rufus (William II), 55, 165*n*18
William I
  reaffirmation of Anglo-Saxon law, 51
Wolsey, Thomas Cardinal
  founding of Royal College, 62
Writing
  origins of, 149*n*2 (chapter 1)
Writs
  in common law, 55
  trespass (trespass on the case), 55
  preoccupation of judges with, 59

Year Book Series
  span (Edward I—Henry VIII), 53
  physicians in, 53